HAIRSPRAY,

FEMALE TROUBLE,

AND MULTIPLE MANIACS

Three MORE Screenplays by JOHN WATERS

THUNDER'S MOUTH PRESS
NEW YORK

John Waters and Divine—close up.

For Matthias Brunner

CONTENTS

HAIRSPRAY, FEMALE TROUBLE, AND MULTIPLE MANIACS
Three More Screenplays by John Waters

Published by
Thunder's Mouth Press
An Imprint of Avalon Publishing Group Inc.

AVALON
publishing group incorporated

Hairspray and Multiple Maniacs on the same bill!? With *Female Trouble* thrown in just to make it a more appallingly confusing package? Tony Award fans of *Hairspray* be warned: it's a long way from David Lochary cooing "I love you so fucking much I could shit" in *Multiple Maniacs* to Ricki Lake's cheery announcement "I'm big, blonde, and beautiful." But think again. Maybe it's not so far after all. Maybe all my movies could be Broadway musicals. Why not write one yourself? Here are three of my favorite "backlist" titles; two haven't been sung yet. Go ahead, write some show tunes to go along with them. Think up some catchy lyrics. Belt 'em out with your friends. Just remember to option the rights.

"Pig fucker," a stranger mumbled to me as he passed me on the street in Manhattan in 2005. Momentarily taken aback, I realized he was merely repeating part of Divine's dialogue from *Multiple Maniacs*, a line I had written myself over thirty-six years ago. God, it feels good to be remembered. *Multiple Maniacs*, my last black-and-white movie and my first with synch-sound. Such a period piece. All that talking (and talking and talking and YELLING!) about "tear gas" and "the pigs" and "the Weathermen." The supposed outrage that a cheeseburger could cost a dollar. Remembering having sex in a movie theater as a normal occurrence. Reminiscing that *Inga* was once a controversial art film.

We were so young when we made this "celluloid atrocity." Mary Vivian Pearce (Bonnie) never imagined then she would survive a brain tumor in 1999. She didn't let it stop her; she's now studying for her master's degree, substitute-teaching in the Baltimore City Public School System, going on bike-riding trips in Vietnam, and she still finds the time to model nude at the Maryland Institute of Art. Mink Stole has lived in Los Angeles for decades and writes an advice column, "Think Mink," for the Baltimore *City Paper*. She works all the time in independent movies and is a great singer, too. One of her smoky ballads, "I Wish I Had a Gun," will be featured on my "A Date with John Waters" compilation CD to be released by New Line Records this year. And Susan Lowe (Suzie, the nympho-"maniac" with hairy armpits who went on to play "Mole" in *Desperate Living*) is a nontraditional grandmother who still paints and sells her work in galleries and on line (suelowe69@yahoo.com). Rick Morrow, the handsome young man who plays Divine's bodyguard "Ricky" in *Maniacs,* is a poet and a cab driver and lives in Springfield, Oregon. Remembering how great Rick looked in the movie wearing a skimpy bathing suit and carrying a gun, I was thrilled recently to discover a wonderful photo of him taken on the set by Lawrence Irvine that shows this young actor in all his off-screen sullen vacant glory.

Vincent Peranio, the production designer for all my films from *Multiple Maniacs* to *A Dirty Shame,* works constantly today ("Homicide," "The Corner," "The Wire") and can be seen onscreen in *Maniacs,* too. He's second from the left in the bottom row of the naked pyramid scene, a cliché pose now forever ruined by the Abu Ghraib prison abuse photos. Pat Moran, my longtime best friend and Emmy Award–winning casting director, who started with me and still works with me today, plays a "straight person" and you can hear her say "I know a couple of queers. In fact, I think my hairdresser's a queer," as she watches "The Cavalcade of Perversion." George Figgs (the junkie-"maniac" who also plays "Christ" in the film) is alive and well and runs a film series at the Creative Alliance in East Baltimore. My old school chum, Bob Skidmore, and his then

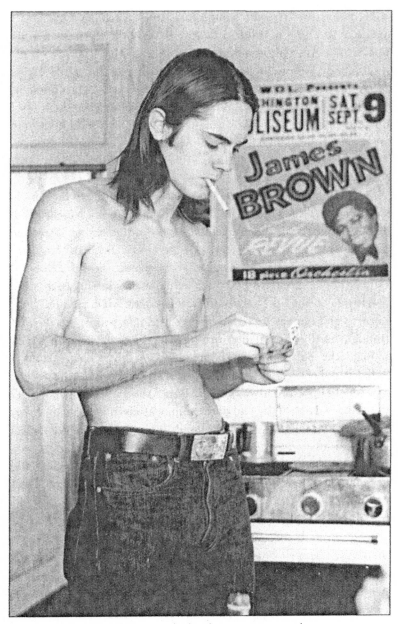

Rick Morrow in my kitchen between camera takes.

wife Margie (the "straight" couple lured into the tent and murdered) are divorced, but I'm still friends with them both. Bob manages the books for retirement homes (I guess *Multiple Maniacs* isn't on his resume) and Margie, remarried, is now a successful tattoo artist. Michael Renner Jr., the child "star" who played "The Infant of Prague," is, of course, an adult, and I wish I knew where he is but I don't. Same with Tom Wells (there—I've actually found his name) who played "The Puke Eater." And Gilbert McGill, the bra-sniffer- "maniac," somewhere he's alive—I hope. I still think of all these people as my friends.

But, God, Ingmar Bergman was right. The "silence" of the dead is sometimes so deafening. Divine, David Lochary, Cookie Mueller, Paul Swift (who made his line-forgetting debut in *Maniacs* as "Steve the Weatherman" and got much better as "The Eggman" in *Pink Flamingos*) and Edith Massey are all in maniac heaven. Howard Gruber and Paul Landis (the "two actual queers kissing each other like lovers on the lips") are both victims of the AIDS plague. Mark Lazarus and Harvey Freed, two other "straight people" in the film (though hardly in real life) are also no longer with us. "Pete's Hotel," the Baltimore flop-house watering hole (Divine always hated it) where Edith Massey really worked, is now a bar called Rodo's (1719 S. Broadway). "Lobstora," the papier-mâché lobster that rapes Divine at the end of the film, was given a burial at sea by Vincent Peranio and me in Baltimore's Inner Harbor before it even had that tourist attraction name.

Nobody had eaten shit yet in my films, but Divine nibbling (and gagging) on a real cow's heart in one scene in *Maniacs* certainly was training-wheels for the finale of *Pink Flamingos*. Foaming at the mouth (easy—Alka-Seltzer without water) was also a warm-up for Divine eventually becoming known as "the filthiest person alive"— on film, at least. And I defy anyone to come up with a more comically sacrilegious scene than the "rosary job" in *Multiple Maniacs*. I was bemused when all the trouble started over Scorsese's *Last Temptation of Christ*. Imagine if the picketers had seen *Multiple Maniacs!* I know Willem Dafoe had seen the "rosary job" but wisely never brought it up when he was promoting his portrayal of Jesus Christ. I was even more delighted to read about Mel Gibson's S&M movie for the whole family, *The Passion of the Christ*. I wanted to go to every screening dressed as the characters and yell out the dialogue like they do in *The Rocky Horror Picture Show*. Both of these supposedly controversial religious movies paled in Jesus-shock-value comparison in my humble opinion.

Rereading the script of *Maniacs*, I'm amazed at how old fashioned I was—my real phone number at the time (235-2354) was mentioned on screen as Divine's. I shot almost entirely on location. Divine and Cookie's "house" was actually my apartment at 315 E. 25th Street, exactly the way it looked in real life. There was no camera "coverage" on any scene as I shot it, just long, long takes where the actors had to repeat pages and pages of dialogue without making a mistake. "Dogma 95"? I guess this was "Dogma 69" (the year we shot *Maniacs*), and I didn't even know it.

And talk about politically incorrect! Besides claiming the Tate-LaBianca murders for her own, Divine names real-life, living movie stars as her future murder victims. Peace and love in the sixties? Ha! *Multiple Maniacs* was a violent call to punk arms before there was a word for it. We may have looked like hippies but that's just so we could sneak up on your sensibilities and mug your sense of humor.

Multiple Maniacs isn't on DVD yet and it's long out of print on video. And yes, we stopped the pirate version that was being mass-produced from a garage in Massachusetts a few years back. With any luck, New Line will re-release it someday. Anyone who feels like nagging them, feel free to write their Home Video and DVD department.

• • •

Female Trouble is my favorite of the Divine "vehicles"; movies shot to showcase his/her extreme beauty. Some of the most popular lines I've written are in this script: "I'd like my hair done quickly and quietly"; "I had some orally, earlier"; "Look in the mirror,

Taffy. For fourteen you don't look so good"; and "I had you tested by a team of doctors and they told me you are most definitely retarded!" Certain dialogue in this film has even become short-hand for veteran Dreamlanders. Anyone who innocently begins a sentence with "Sometimes I wish . . .", we (yes, I mean it royally) cut them off with the snotty comeback line from the film "Well, throw a goddamn penny in a fountain and make a goddamn wish and maybe it will come true." And anytime a friend makes up an obviously phony excuse for a physical injury, we always go back to Divine's lying cover-up for a black eye, "I fell and hit my eye on the farebox (of a bus)." Oh, sure.

Pre-mustache (1969).

Of course, time changes everything that once was topical. Inflation rears its ugly head again in *Female Trouble* when the $104 price tag for a hairdo is meant to be ridiculously high. The *New York Times* recently wrote about the routine acceptance of a $600 haircut in some neighborhoods in Manhattan, making this joke in the script obsolete. The "crime is beauty" theme brings up a lot of notorious criminals of the time; some have fared better than others in the lasting-fame department. Richard Speck, the notorious mass murderer of seven Chicago nurses, is still remembered in horror, but the jailhouse videotape that surfaced after his death showing him with the giant silicone breasts he had somehow gotten in prison may out-shock his original crimes. Arthur Bremer (would-be assassin of George Wallace and author of *An Assassin's Diary*) is almost finished serving his thirty-year sentence in Maryland, and, according to a friend who was in jail with him for decades, "he's still nutty as a fruitcake." Abbie Hoffman may have had a tragic end to his life but trouble-makers of a certain age wish he were still here—think what he and the Yippies could do with the Bush presidency.

Alice Crimmins, the Long Island mother accused and acquitted of murdering her two children, was a tabloid queen who screamed "Liar, liar!" to the prosecution witnesses. Her courtroom theatrics inflamed the press and public alike and were a major influence on my writing the character of Dawn Davenport (the murdering heroine of *Female Trouble*). Alice Crimmins is free today, living somewhere below the Court TV radar, but I'll never forget her. Through an old friend, I now know the current editor of *Newsday*, the paper that really made her a star, and every summer when I see him I badger him to find Alice and do an update. Alice Crimmins, I miss you!

And Leslie Bacon, the supposed Weatherman sympathizer who was falsely accused of having "personal knowledge" of the March 1, 1971, bombing of the U.S. Capitol? She is completely forgotten today. At one time in the seventies, I had heard that she was, at first, mad that Divine mentioned her in the "crime-rant" nightclub scene, but after seeing *Female Trouble*, supposedly she had laughed. I don't know if that's true, but Leslie Bacon, I still love you and hope you're doing well these days.

Female Trouble is loaded with germs of ideas that became full-fledged diseases in my later showbiz life. The anti-sex rants of Donald and Donna (David Lochary and Mary Vivian Pearce) precede the Neuters' hatred of eros in *A Dirty Shame* and Divine's shooting up for real on film was a reality TV scene before its time. Swimming across a river in full drag in a November sleet storm might be something Johnny Knoxville would have done on his "Jackass" TV show.

The roll-call of the dead is most severe in *Female Trouble*: Divine, David Lochary, Cookie Mueller, Paul Swift, Edith Massey, Seymour Avigdor (Dawn's defense lawyer), and even the beloved Chris Mason (Dreamland hairdresser from *Female Trouble* to *Cry-Baby*) who doubled as Matron #1 ("bumping pussies is a violation of jail rules!").

Hilary Taylor, who played Taffy as a child, is alive and well and showed up at a college lecture I gave. Even though she is now a grown woman, she looked exactly the same! I took her up on stage with me and the audience went wild. I've lost track of Gator (Michael Potter), but when I had my first meeting with Johnny Depp, he mentioned "Gator's performance" as a reason why he wanted to make a film with me. The last time I saw Michael, he showed up on the set of *Hairspray* looking radically different. I guess being married to Divine (even if only in a movie) can cause severe lifestyle changes.

• • •

When *Hairspray*, the Broadway musical version of my film, won the Tony, I suppressed the urge to immediately begin wearing ascots. But when the MPAA gave the original film a PG rating, I thought my fans would kill me. I had accidentally made a feel-good movie and I didn't even know it. Divine's death a week after the film opened gives me a hole in my memory—I can't remember the joy I must have had for the few days the film had been well reviewed and its star was basking in newfound glory.

Rereading the script (other possible titles at the time: "White Lipstick," "Shake a Tailfeather," "Hairhoppers"), I see that Tracy Turnblad, our chubby heroine (Ricki Lake) had a dark side that was wisely cut out of the final product. In the shooting script, Tracy is forced to work in her father Wilber's (Jerry Stiller) joke shop and, in a rage of defiance, humiliates a dorkish customer in front of her horrified parents. "She's on cough medicine," her mother Edna (Divine) worries out loud. "Thanks for not buying anything!" Tracy yells as the appalled customer runs from the shop.

Tracy was racy, too: getting a hickey at a Corny Collins record hop from a male hunk, and after telling Penny (Leslie Ann Powers) "I did let him dry-hump my leg," worrying that he might have "blue balls." Would "Blue Balls" have been a Broadway show tune if this line hadn't been cut from the film?

In another scene, Tracy rescues Link (Michael St. Gerard) from a rumble by spraying hairspray in the eyes of his attacker. She even threatens her parents that she's going to "run away to Mississippi and become a freedom fighter." But the most surprising of the cut scenes shows Tracy (after shoplifting a pair of shoes) breaking into archrival Amber's (Colleen Fitzgerald—who later became the pop star "Vitamin C") house and dyeing her hair blond as she snoops through Amber's diary and roots through her closets. I remember Bob Shaye, New Line's head-honcho and the executive producer of the film, watching the first cut of *Hairspray* with the scene where Tracy actually did have real roaches in her hair (Ricki Lake still bitches about that day). "What is this?" he bellowed, "a Buñuel film?!"

Whole dance numbers got cut, too: "The Push 'n' Kick," "The Stupidity" (you danced like a spastic). And a few good lines bit the dust with them ("Link, please don't look at my legs without the benefit of nylons"). A subplot concerning Nadine's (Dawn Hill) racial anger at the white integration sympathizers strayed too far from the main characters and ended up on the cutting room floor. Vincent Peranio, the production designer, still wishes the set of "Nadine's Basement" had seen the light of day.

Maybe I'll revive some of these scenes when I do the "Peyton Place"–type TV soap opera version of *Hairspray* long after the movie of the Broadway musical, the road companies, and the high school productions have finally played out. Just think: "The Corny Collins Show" is cancelled by the TV station—now what? Tracy becomes a speed freak, Link turns gay, Penny gets an abortion, Seaweed joins the Black Panthers, Motormouth is busted for payola, Corny is falsely accused of child molesting, and Amber gets a facelift that goes bad. Every time I mention these ideas to Margo Lion, one of the producers of *Hairspray* the musical, she turns white and begs me to reconsider.

NEW LINE CINEMA
PRESENTS

IN ASSOCIATION WITH STANLEY F. BUCHTHAL
A JOHN WATERS FILM

HAIRSPRAY

A star is born (Ricki Lake).

WRITTEN AND DIRECTED BY JOHN WATERS

Producer . . . . RACHEL TALALAY
Executive Producers . . . . ROBERT SHAYE and SARA RISHER
Co-producers . . . . STANLEY F. BUCHTHAL and JOHN WATERS
Line Producer . . . . ROBERT MAIER
Director of Photography . . . . DAVID INSLEY
Editor . . . . JANICE HAMPTON
Hair Design . . . . CHRISTINE MASON
Costume and Makeup Design . . . . VAN SMITH
Art Director . . . . VINCE PERANIO
Casting Director . . . . MARY COLQUHOUN
Casting Director Baltimore . . . . PAT MORAN
Choreographer . . . . EDWARD LOVE

STARRING
(in alphabetical order)
Franklin Von Tussle . . . . SONNY BONO
Motormouth Maybelle . . . . RUTH BROWN
Edna Turnblad . . . . DIVINE
Arvin Hodgepile . . . . DIVINE
Amber Von Tussle . . . . COLLEEN FITZPATRICK
Link Larkin . . . . MICHAEL ST. GERARD
Velma Von Tussle . . . . DEBBIE HARRY
Tracy Turnblad . . . . RICKI LAKE
Penny Pingleton . . . . LESLIE ANN POWERS
Seaweed . . . . CLAYTON PRINCE
Wilbur Turnblad . . . . JERRY STILLER
Tammy . . . . MINK STOLE
Corny Collins . . . . SHAWN THOMPSON
Beatnik Cat . . . . RIC OCASEK
Beatnik Girl . . . . PIA ZADORA

COUNCIL MEMBERS

Iggy . . . . JOSH CHARLES
Bobby . . . . JASON DOWNS
IQ . . . . HOLTER FORD GRAHAM
Brad . . . . DAN GRIFFITH
Pam . . . . REGINA HAMMOND
Consuella . . . . BRIDGET KIMSEY
Dash . . . . FRANKIE MALDON
Lou Ann . . . . BROOKE MILLS
Fender . . . . JOHN OROFINO
Carmelita . . . . KIM WEBB
Shelly . . . . DEBRA WIRTH

AND

Nadine . . . . DAWN HILL
L'il Inez . . . . CYRKLE MILBOURNE
Mr. Pinky . . . . ALAN WENDL
Prudence Pingleton . . . . JOANN HAVRILLA
Governor . . . . LEO ROCCA
Dr. Fredrikson . . . . JOHN WATERS
Himself . . . . TOUSSAINT MCCALL
Gym Teacher . . . . KATHLEEN WALLACE
Lead Lafayette . . . . KEITH DOUGLAS

1) Exterior WZZT-TV studio. 1962. Baltimore, Maryland. The original title song "Hairspray," sung by Rachel Sweet, plays over the credits.

2) Interior WZZT-TV. "The Corny Collins Show" set. Fifty-some TEENAGERS are about ready to go on dance party TV show. They are dressed in extreme fashions of the day. Girls with giant bouffant hairdos, cat-eye makeup, white lipstick, angel blouses, black nylons, pointy-toed cha-cha heels. Boys with pegged pants, skinny ties, buckled chuck-a-boots, sport coats with belts on the back, and "D.A.," "waterfall," and "Detroit" haircuts.

CORNY COLLINS, a thirtyish brash DJ type, is already on set looking through 45-rpm records, deciding what to play. When nobody's looking, he throws out a Pat Boone record.

Corny's assistant director, TAMMY, a no-nonsense kind of gal in her mid-thirties, is lecturing the TV CAMERMAN about his upcoming shots.

IQ JONES, a hoody, cute teen regular on the show, is lovingly spit-shining, his pointy-toed shoes.

LOU ANN LEVOROWSKI, his trashy teen co-star with a "double-bubble" hairdo, sprays her coif while eating potato chips.

BOBBY, a young boy greaser, expertly practices the "Mashed Potato" dance.

CONSUELLA, a tiny girl with an "airlift" hairdo, sneakily puts falsies under her sweater and adjusts them.

CARMELITA, an older teen who's been on the show for years, applies white lipstick.

PAM and BRAD, a popular couple on the show, are cuddling on set. They accidentally mess up each other's hair and then spray it back into place.

DASH, a dreamboat teen, uses the TV camera lens as a mirror to fix his hair. Wetting his fingers with saliva, he also combs his eyelashes in the right direction.

SHELLY, a fifteen-year-old hair-hopper, applies bottom eyeliner like a pro.

IGGY and FENDER, two "continental" heartthrobs, use the reflection on the top of a Pepsi cooler to primp before the show begins.

AMBER VON TUSSLE, the stuck-up blonde pineapple princess and the most popular ingénue on the show, is seen sneakily changing the results on the "1962 Miss Auto Show" vote tabulation board so she is further in the lead.

LINK LARKIN, Amber's handsome, Fabian look-alike boyfriend, the most popular guy on the show, sprays his pompadour with hairspray and moans in almost erotic pleasure.

TAMMY

Okay. Places! Sixty seconds to air time! No chewing gum! And, for God's sake, smile! Look *happy* to be on "The Corny Collins Show"! Forty-five seconds.

Credits end. Title song ends.

3) Exterior East Baltimore blue-collar neighborhood. We hear Dee-Dee Sharp's "Mashed Potatoes" on soundtrack. School bus pulls up and lets KIDS out. Exit TRACY TURNBLAD, an overweight but pretty sixteen-year-old who wears an extreme teased hairdo. Following closely behind her is fourteen-year-old PENNY PINGLETON, not nearly as worldly as TRACY, but trying hard to imitate the cool girls of the early sixties. They race up the street of identical row houses, past endless white marble steps, with HOUSEWIVES diligently scrubbing them, to Tracy's house—a corner row house next to Hardy-Har Joke Shop, her parents' business.

4) Interior TV studio. "Mashed Potatoes" is still playing for warm-up.

TAMMY

Thirty seconds to air time! Lou Ann, if I see you doing the "Dirty Boogie" even once, you're off the show!

Cameras are being positioned, CONTROL ROOM CREWS are in place.

TAMMY
(Frantically)
Council members! I see guests without partners! Shelly, your bra-strap is showing! IQ, put a tie around that lovely little neck before I wring it! Twenty seconds!

5) Interior Turnblad house. Living room. Lower-middle class, but incredibly neat. Late 1950s furniture. Plastic slipcovers. We see EDNA TURN-BLAD, Tracy's mother, a stout woman, dressed in late 1950s housedress with long, hillbilly hairdo. EDNA is behind ironing board while MRS. MALINSKI, a neighbor, leaves bags of ironing and pays for clothes she picks up. TRACY and PENNY run in.

TRACY
(Routinely)
I'm home!

PENNY
(Removing "red-hot fireball" and fanning her mouth to speak, something she does frequently throughout the film.)
Afternoon, Miss Edna.

"More soiled laundry for Mommy" (Divine).

EDNA
Penny, your mother called . . .

TRACY and PENNY rush out.

EDNA
(Continuing)
Tracy Turnblad, can't you say hello to Mrs. Malinski?
(Shaking her head in worry; to MRS. MALINSKI)
Everyday, she's gotta watch "The Corny Collins Show."

MRS. MALINSKI
Delinquents, if you ask me. It ain't right bein' on TV and dancing
to colored music.

EDNA
(Annoyed)
She's *just* a teenager.

6) *Interior Turnblad's rec room. Cut to TRACY flicking on giant TV console to catch credits and opening number of "The Corny Collins Show." "Mashed Potatoes" is playing. Cut back and forth from TV studio with KIDS doing gimmick dance "Mashed Potatoes" to PENNY and TRACY wildly doing the same steps along with the show.*

7) *Interior Turnblad kitchen.*

EDNA
Could you turn that racket down?! I'm *trying* to iron in here!

8) *Interior TV studio. "Mashed Potatoes" ends. Everybody claps.*

VOICE-OVER
Ladies and Gentlemen, Corny Collins!!

CORNY COLLINS *is seated behind his DJ desk. A "Top 20" board is behind him.*

CORNY
Hello, Baltimore, and welcome to "The Corny Collins Show"!

KIDS applaud.

> CORNY
> *(Continuing)*
> That was DeeDee Sharp and today's bulls-eye hit "Mashed Potato Time"! And, hey, we've got our first telegram of the day!
> *(Reaching over and pulling off telegram from giant machine next to desk)*
> "Please have Lou Ann Levorowski and IQ Jones lead a dance. Signed your number one fan in West Baltimore."

LOU ANN and IQ are signaled by TAMMY to come on camera next to CORNY.

> LOU ANN
> Hi, Corny!

> IQ
> *(To camera)*
> Hi, West Baltimore!

> CORNY
> Lou Ann, you're a groovy chick. How long have you been a regular on the show?

> LOU ANN
> I've been on the Council for five months.

> CORNY
> And you, IQ?

> IQ
> Two outa-sight years!

KIDS applaud.

9) *Interior Turnblad's rec room. TRACY and PENNY are mesmerized by TV.*

> TRACY
> God, he's gorgeous, Penny.

PENNY
(In awe)
Look at her hair. It's a "split level." She's so beautiful. She's my
favorite Council Member on the show.

10) *Interior TV studio.*

CORNY
And what's your favorite record from The Survey?

IQ and LOU ANN
"GRAVY"!

CORNY
(As the record begins)
Lou Ann Levorowski and IQ Jones leading our next dance! "Give
Me Gravy on My Mashed Potatoes"!

EVERYONE *on show claps to the beat as* IQ *and* LOU ANN *break into
the* "Gravy" *dance, similar to* "Mashed Potatoes" *only with pouring
motions with the hands.*

11) *Interior Turnblad's rec room. TRACY and PENNY dance as TRACY
demonstrates intricate "pouring" motion to an eager PENNY.*

12) *Interior TV studio. All KIDS join in dancing "Gravy" when TAMMY
gives the off camera signal. TAMMY then holds up "Tilted Acres" cue
card and begins signaling to AMBER, who discretely "gravies" her way
off dance floor with LINK and over to "set" for "Tilted Acres Amusement
Park." Set consists of roller-coaster car at top of ten-foot track leading
down to TV camera position. LINK helps AMBER up ladder and she gets
in coaster car, nervously fixing hair and checking makeup before she goes
on. "Gravy" ends and KIDS clap. Cut to shot of AMBER, hands in the
air, screaming as car is released down the track and hits camera position.*

AMBER
(To camera)
Hi! I'm Amber Von Tussle, a Corny Collins Council Member, and I
just *love* Tilted Acres Amusement Park! And, remember, this year's
grand opening—Wednesday, June 1st. All rides! All day! For just
one dollar! The Wild Mouse, The Round-Up, The Salt and Pepper

Shaker, The Whip! Tilted Acres! Where the screaming . . .
(Screams theatrically)
. . . never stops!

13) *Interior Turnblad's rec room.*

TRACY
(Watching intently)
I hate her! She thinks she's hot shit!

PENNY
She's a rich bitch and the only reason she got on the show is her parents *own* Tilted Acres.

14) *Interior TV studio. CORNY approaches AMBER on camera, helps her from coaster car and they walk to "Conversation Corner," a part of the cheesy set where Council Members are sometimes interviewed. A bag of fan mail is spread out on the table.*

CORNY
(Sitting down)
All for you, Amber! The most popular girl on the show!

AMBER sits and affectedly throws fan mail in the air, squealing.

CORNY
(Continuing)
It's no secret that you're one of the top contestants in our 1962 Miss Auto Show Contest. I thought you'd like to be the first to see today's election results.

SHELLY, another Council Member, wheels out giant, home-made graph, with the names Amber, Lou Ann, Shelly, Carmelita, Consuella, etc., with changeable bars representing the number of votes.

CORNY
(Continuing)
Who will be the lucky lady from the Corny Collins Council to be named queen? Only you, the home viewers, can decide by filling in your ballot and mailing it today!
(Eyeballing results)
Amber, there's no stoppin' ya—you're leading by over 1100 votes!

AMBER
(Squeals in happiness)
If elected, I promise to be a teen-queen all of Baltimore will be proud of.

15) Interior Turnblad's rec room.

TRACY
(Watching Amber, making gagging noises)
The stuck-up little spastic.

PENNY
(Repulsed)
She's such a queer.

16) Interior TV studio.

CORNY
Congratulations, Amber. And now the question everybody at home is asking: Are you still going steady with Link?

AMBER
(Flashing wax-filled ring)
Yes, I am, Corny. Link and I have been going together for sixteen months. We *met* on the show!

CROWD applauds. TAMMY shoves LINK on camera.

CORNY
Ah, here comes the handsome devil now. Link, why don't you tell the home audience where we are going to be tonight?

LINK
Well, Corny, we're going to be at Unity Hall Dundalk Teen Center . . .

AMBER
. . . for the Corny Collins Record Hop.

CORNY
(To camera)
And each and every one of you is invited. So come on out, dance to
the hits, meet your favorite Council Members and don't be late!
Unity Hall. Eight o'clock.
(To AMBER)
What do you want to hear, Amber?

AMBER
"Shake a Tail Feather" by the Five Du-Tones!

*Music begins—"Shake a Tail Feather." AMBER and LINK do wild ver-
sion as KIDS clap.*

*17) Interior Turnblad's rec room. Cut back and forth between AMBER and
LINK dancing in a studio and TRACY and PENNY in rec room. The song
becomes a battle as TRACY shakes her tail feather at AMBER on TV show.*

PENNY
(Singing)
Shake it! Shake it! Shake it, Baby!

TRACY
(Singing)
Here we go loopdy-loop!
(To PENNY)
Oh, God, I love this record!

PENNY
You should be on that Council, not her!

TRACY
I know I should, Penny. I'm going to that hop tonight!

PENNY
Oh, let me come! We'll lie and say we're going to the library to study.

TRACY
It's a deal. We'll meet eight o'clock sharp. Up on the Avenue.

*TRACY and PENNY go into a frenzy of dancing. EDNA glares from
doorway. She marches over and turns off the TV.*

EDNA
Okay, young ladies. I've had about *enough* of that screeching music!

TRACY
(Haughtily)
Mother, we're *watching* "The Corny Collins Show"!

EDNA
Penny, your mother called, all frantic. She said you were punished.

PENNY
(Whining)
I'm always punished.

EDNA
And Tracy, I've told you about that hair! All ratted up like a teenage jezebel!

TRACY
Oh, mother, you're so fifties!

PENNY
Tracy's "double-bubble" is all the rage, Miss Edna. Jackie Kennedy, our First Lady, even rats her hair.

EDNA
Tracy ain't no first lady, are you, Tracy? No siree, she's a hair-hopper, that's what she is. Now, I've got nothing but hampers of ironing to do and my diet pill is wearing off. Tracy, I want you to go to your room and study. And Penny, don't be listening to every bit of nonsense my daughter tells you. If I didn't know better, I'd swear she was mental.

Knock is heard at door.

EDNA
(Continuing)
. . . Now what?
(Going to answer it)
More soiled laundry for Mommy, I suppose!

EDNA opens door to reveal hysterical MRS. PINGLETON, Penny's mother, who rushes in house.

> MRS. PINGLETON
>
> Edna, have you seen Penny?

> EDNA
>
> Good lord Prudy, she's right here.

> PENNY
> *(Wearily)*
>
> Hi, Mom.

> MRS. PINGLETON
>
> Penny Pingleton, you know you were punished! From now on, you're wearing a giant "P" on your blouse every day to school so the whole world knows Penny Pingleton is Permanently, Positively Punished!

MRS. PINGLETON grabs PENNY by the arm.

> PENNY
>
> Bye, Miss Edna.

> TRACY
> *(Mouthing the words to PENNY)*
>
> Eight o'clock!

MRS. PINGLETON drags her daughter out, slamming the door behind her.

18) *Wipe to Exterior WZZT. The show has ended and COUNCIL MEM-BERS are exiting, being mobbed by teenage FANS, clutching autograph books and offerings for their favorite "stars." We hear "I Wish I Were a Princess" by Little Peggy March on soundtrack as AMBER and LINK walk out. The FANS go nuts, yelling, "You're beautiful," "I love your hair." AMBER and LINK run to Amber's flashy 1962 sports car and peel out, as FANS chase in teen worship.*

19) *Shot of LINK and AMBER pulling up in front of her family's house, "the richest home in East Baltimore," a home improvement nightmare. They park and make out passionately. AMBER glances in rearview mirror, notices a small pimple and panics, hastily saying goodbye to LINK, shoving him out of her car.*

. . . and after.

Velma Von Tussle (Debbie Harry)
before . . .

AMBER
(Sobbing)
I happen to have a blemish!

AMBER runs into her house, leaving a confused LINK in the street.

20) Interior Von Tussle home. Nouveau-riche, early sixties, hilariously "plush" interior. Amber's mother, VELMA VON TUSSLE, an overly dressed, lacquered and made-up fuss-budget, anxiously awaits her daughter. AMBER enters.

VELMA
You had three good closeups today. Period! Can't you dance up front where the voters can *see* you?

AMBER
(Running up steps to her room)
Mother! I have a pimple.

VELMA
(Following her)
And you *had* to pick a colored record as your favorite song, didn't you? That's nice for the neighbors! You got something against Connie Francis? Shelley Fabares?

21) Interior Amber's bedroom. Decorated in ultimate frilly, 1962 teenage cute. Annette Funicello posters, ridiculous stuffed animals, and stacks of fan mail fill the room. AMBER is seated at her ornate makeup table staring at blemish in ridiculously large magnifying glass.

VELMA
(Entering)
You know if your father is forced to integrate Tilted Acres, we're out of business. Can't you at least *act* white on television?

AMBER
Leave me alone, mother! "Shake a Tail Feather" is a wild song—it's got a good beat and you can dance to it.
(Looking back in mirror)
Oh, God, of all nights. A Corny Collins record hop and I've got CRATERS!

VELMA
(Sitting next to her, examining it)
You can barely even see it.

AMBER
(Having a fit)
Where's my Clearasil?! Get me some alcohol!
(Bursting into tears)
I have ACNE!! POP IT! PLEASE POP IT!

VELMA
(Rushing around, taking over, getting rubber gloves)
Don't be ridiculous. Lie down!

AMBER lies on bed and VELMA "operates" on her.

VELMA
(Continuing)
Your skin is beautiful, Amber. So creamy. So white. But every oily, greasy potato chip you pop in your gullet is a potential whitehead. And we all know what comes after whiteheads. IMPETIGO!
(Popping pimple)
There! It's gone. Now it's time for you know what!

AMBER
Mother, I know all the dances!

VELMA
Come on, get up! Practice makes perfect. I ought to know. Don't forget, I was "Miss Soft Crab" in 1945 and that title wasn't handed to me on a silver platter. I worked for it! Come on, a one, a two, a three . . . Pony!

AMBER leaps up for "drill" and does a "Pony" dance.

VELMA
(Continuing)
"Mashed Potatoes"! Faster!

AMBER *mechanically performs each dance her mother calls.*

> VELMA
> *(Continuing)*
> Give me "Gravy"!!

> AMBER
> *(Doing it)*
> I *did* that on the show today!

> VELMA
> Turkey Trot!!

FRANKLIN VON TUSSLE, *Amber's father, enters. He wears a hideous green suit and carries a stack of fliers.*

> FRANKLIN
> Amber, honey, I'd like to talk to you.

> AMBER
> Yes, daddy?

> VELMA
> Don't stop! Cha-cha!

> AMBER
> *(Obeying)*
> I'm tired!

> VELMA
> One, two! Cha-cha-cha!

> FRANKLIN
> *(Beaming)*
> I had some new campaign fliers printed up today . . . All for daddy's little darlin'.

FRANKLIN *shows handbill with Amber's photo and headline "LET AMBER TAKE YOU FOR A FREE RIDE."*

FRANKLIN
(Continuing)
I want you to hand these out tonight at the hop. Each and every one
of them.

VELMA
TWIST!

AMBER
(Twisting)
Oh, Daddy!

VELMA
(Grabbing her twisting daughter)
No lip from you, Miss Ingrate! This campaign is costing us an arm
and a leg!

FRANKLIN
New gowns, hairdresser three times a week. Why, your hairspray
bill alone eats up all the profits from the Tilt-A-Whirl.

VELMA
You'll do as Daddy says or we'll send you to Catholic School where
you belong!

22) *Wipe to Interior Turnblad's kitchen. WILBUR, Tracy's father, who is
dressed in a loud sports shirt and baggy trousers, has just finished a meat
loaf dinner with EDNA. TRACY is still eating ferociously.*

TRACY
(To EDNA)
Pass the macaroni and cheese.

EDNA frowns.

TRACY
(Continuing)
PLEASE!

A growing girl needs food (Ricki Lake).

EDNA
(Passing the bowl)
Didn't you take that appetite suppressant I gave you on Dr. McKenzie's orders?

TRACY
I'm a growing teenager. I *need* food.

WILBUR
Let her eat, Edna.
(To TRACY)
Tracy, did you do your chores around the house today?

EDNA
Not Miss Tracy—Cyd Charisse herself! She's too busy ratting her hair and doing the Ubangi Stomp.

WILBUR
Tracy, we all have responsibilities in life. You may think owning the Hardy-Har Joke Shop is all drudgery—unwrapping Dribble Glasses, checking Dog-E-Doo inventory, but I love it. You'll see, work can be fun!

TRACY
(Rudely)
Can I be excused to go to the library to study?

EDNA
Do you purposefully 'forget everything we tell you?

WILBUR
(To TRACY)
Remember? It's June 1st. Your first night behind the counter at the Hardy-Har!
(To EDNA, optimistically)
Get out your baby book and mark the date—Tracy's got a job!

TRACY
(Jumping up)
I hate that stupid store! Wait 'til I tell my guidance counselor that I'm not allowed to study. No! I have to work on a chain gang.

EDNA
You heard your father. March!

23) Interior Hardy-Har Joke Shop. Every conceivable practical joke is displayed. WILBUR, EDNA, and TRACY enter. KID CUSTOMERS are outside waiting to enter.

WILBUR
(To KIDS)
We'll be open in a second.
(To TRACY)
Now, first, I want you to get familiar with some of our best-selling products.
(Picks up novelty item)
This is the handshake buzzer. First you wind it up . . .
(Doing it)
. . . and then . . . let me show you. Come on, shake.

TRACY hesitates.

EDNA
Do it, or no TV all week!

TRACY sticks out hand to shake and buzzer goes off.

> **WILBUR**
>
> Ha ha ha ha! See?! "Hardy har har har!" you should say. That gets customers in the mood to buy!

> **TRACY**
>
> You're sick.

> **WILBUR**
>
> I bet you're just tired. Have a seat . . .

TRACY looks suspicious.

> **WILBUR**
> *(Continuing)*
> Go on, get a load off your feet.

> **EDNA**
>
> You want a smack?

TRACY sits down and rude farting sound is heard.

> **WILBUR**
>
> P-U!! What did you have, beans for dinner?! Hardy har har!

> **EDNA**
>
> Hardy har har har!

> **WILBUR**
>
> Go ahead . . . say it.

> **TRACY**
>
> I won't . . .

> **WILBUR**
>
> Lighten up, Tracy, can't you take a joke?
> *(Reaching under seat and pulling out Whoopie Cushion)*
> See? It's a Whoopie Cushion, our number-one best seller! Hardy har har har! Come on, practice!

TRACY

I'd rather die first.

EDNA

Say it or no library. Hardy har har har!

WILBUR

She's just shy, Edna. Go ahead, let the customers in. Tracy, get behind the counter.

EDNA opens door and CHILDREN rush in.

WILBUR
(Continuing)
Hardy har har har, kids!

KIDS
(Happily)
Hardy har har har, Mr. Turnblad.

Eleven year-old GIRL nerd rushes over to TRACY. WILBUR and EDNA watch nervously.

GIRL

Do you have any itching powder?

TRACY

How would you like it if somebody did that to you?

GIRL

Well . . . I just thought it would be funny.

TRACY

You thought wrong. It's stupid just like you are.

TRACY grabs bottle marked "Disappearing Ink" and throws contents on girl's outfit.

TRACY
(Continuing)
Oh . . . excuse me!

                    GIRL
              (Crying out)
My school blouse! You've ruined my good school blouse!

GIRL runs out.

                    TRACY
Can't you take a joke?
              (Looking defiantly at stunned parents)
How my doin'?

An approaching BOY looks at ice cube with flies in it.

                    TRACY
              (Continuing)
Can I help you with something?

                    BOY
              (Excitedly)
Boy, my little sister would have a cow if she found one of these in
her orange juice. How much?

                    TRACY
They're not for sale!
              (Grabbing joke chewing gum pack off shelf)
How about this? Want some gum?

                    BOY
No . . . I . . . wanted . . .

                    TRACY
Take it!

*BOY hesitates, pulls stick of gum from trick pack and has his finger
snapped loudly by mechanism. He howls and tries to pull stick of gum off
finger.*

                    TRACY
              (Continuing)
Real funny, huh?

BOY *runs crying out of joke shop.*

> BOY
> My finger! She broke my finger!

> EDNA
> *(To WILBUR)*
> She's high on cough medicine . . .

> WILBUR
> Tracy . . . please!!

> TRACY
> I'm with a customer, Daddy!

TRACY *approaches third CUSTOMER who is cowering from her.*

> TRACY
> *(Continuing)*
> Gimme all your money! Now!

> CUSTOMER
> *(Running from store)*
> Nooooooo!

> TRACY
> *(Calling after him)*
> Thanks for not buying anything!
> *(To appalled parents)*
> Hardy har har har har har! *Now,* can I go to the library and study?

24) *Wipe to Exterior Unity Hall. KIDS are filing into the Corny Collins record hop, which is in progress. We hear Chubby Checker's "Dancin' Party" on soundtrack.*

25) *Interior Unity Hall. Kids wildly dancing on large dance floor. Folding chairs around the walls. CORNY sits at makeshift DJ booth, sorting through 45s while TAMMY watches KIDS like a hawk.*

26) *Interior Entrance Unity Hall. A SECURITY GUARD is frisking arriving TEENAGERS. Behind him is a table full of liquor bottles and*

weapons taken from other KIDS. TRACY and PENNY rush in and take their place in line behind a clean-cut BLACK TEEN COUPLE. The SECURITY GUARD blocks the black teen couple's entrance.

                    BLACK MALE TEEN
What's the problem, Officer?

                    SECURITY GUARD
This is a white establishment.

                    BLACK FEMALE TEEN
                (Not believing her ears)
Oh, come on . . .

                    BLACK MALE TEEN
We just came to dance . . .

BLACK TEEN COUPLE leaves in defeat.

                    TRACY
                (To SECURITY GUARD)
Hey, that's not fair.

27) Interior Unity Hall. AMBER notices TRACY at the entrance and laughs and whispers rude comments to her boyfriend, LINK. Song ends.

                    CORNY
Boys and girls, stay on the dance floor! Here comes the hottest dance today, and it started right here in Baltimore!

KIDS applaud.

                    CORNY
                (Continuing)
And where did you see it, kids?

                    KIDS
                (In unison)
"The Corny Collins Show"!

CORNY

A big strong line! Ladies and Gentlemen, it's MADISON TIME!

KIDS applaud wildly.

Entire COUNCIL plus a few adventurous "outside" DANCERS take their places, four lines deep, and begin the great, complicated dance "The Madison." LINK and AMBER are right up front. All the KIDS gawk at their favorite "stars." TRACY is wide-eyed, ready to dance, and boldly butts her way into the "Madison" line and starts doing the steps ("Wilt Chamberlain Hook," "T-Time," "Cleveland Box," and "Jackie Gleason") with amazing skill. CORNY and TAMMY immediately notice this new dancer. PENNY is beaming with pride. AMBER looks peeved, but LINK is impressed with Tracy's skill. FENDER, the ladies' man, is craning his neck to get a better look at the "new girl." Song ends and TEENS applaud happily.

CORNY
(Continuing)
Okay, cool teens, before we move on, I've got an emergency announcement to make.
(Reading)
"If Penny Pingleton is in the hall, please call your mother immediately."

Everyone laughs as PENNY freezes in total mortification. TRACY runs protectively towards her.

CORNY
(Continuing)
Now, hold on to your hats all you Continental rockers, 'cause it's dance contest time! And we've got the WILDEST judge in town! You listen to her every night on WEDD! And she hosts "Negro Day" on "The Corny Collins Show" the last Thursday of each month. Let's have a big, warm welcome for the Queen of Baltimore Soul—Motormouth Maybelle herself!

KIDS go wild. MOTORMOUTH MAYBELLE, a big-boned black DJ with bleached-blond hair, comes on stage dressed in an outlandishly theatrical outfit.

MOTORMOUTH

Ooooh, Tiddley Papa! I am a whopper! Motormouth Maybelle's
the name and dancin' is my game!

CORNY

Okay, Motormouth! You're the judge!

MOTORMOUTH

Yip, dip, dip, dip! Yeah! Yeah! Yip, dip, dip, dip! Yeah! Yeah!
Motormouth, Motormouth, Motormouth!

CORNY

Chubby Checker! Pony Time!!

FENDER *grabs* TRACY *as his partner.* PENNY *is asked by* ANTON.
AMBER *picks a* GUEST *who we've seen is a good dancer.*

AMBER
(Whispering snidely to TRACY)
Okay, fatso, let's see what you're made of.

TRACY *is enraged, but "Pony Time" starts and all* DANCERS *begin
competing.* MOTORMOUTH *goes through crowd, eliminating COU-
PLES by tapping them on the shoulder.* PENNY *and* ANTON *are one of
the first to go.* TRACY *and* FENDER *aggressively "Pony" as* AMBER
and GUEST *do the same. Each does the "galloping" steps with hostility
toward the other. Finally, all* COUPLES *are eliminated but three:* AMBER
and GUEST, TRACY *and* FENDER, *and a* THIRD COUPLE.

CORNY

Well, Motormouth, just three couples left. Couple number one, we
all know you, Amber Von Tussle.

AMBER

Future Miss Auto Show!

CORNY

Who's your partner, Amber?

BRENT

I'm Brent from Remington.

MOTORMOUTH
(Moving on to next couple)
Couple Number Two, you look so new. You want some fame?
What's your name?

CLINTON
I'm Clinton from Middle River.

AMY
I'm Amy from Armistead Gardens. I listen to you every night,
Motormouth!

CORNY
(Moving to TRACY and FENDER)
I noticed this girl lookin' good in the Madison Line!

TRACY
Tracy Turnblad, and I'm from Highlandtown.

MOTORMOUTH
This child is wild!

CORNY
Hey, Fender, how long have you been on the show?

FENDER
Two years, one month, and sixteen days!

CORNY
Kids, now it's up to you. IQ, bring on the applause meter.

IQ brings out ludicrous, jerry-rigged applause meter.

CORNY
(Holding hand over AMBER and GUEST)
Couple Number One.

Big applause—hand on scale flies up.

CORNY
(Continuing)
Couple Number Two!

Lukewarm response—hand barely moves.

CORNY
(Continuing)
Couple Number Three!

Biggest applause—hand flies up, over the top for TRACY and FENDER.

CORNY
(Continuing)
The winners are . . .

MOTORMOUTH
Yip, dip, dip, dip.
(Making car revving noises)
Brmmm. Brmmm. Brmmm. Brmmm. I love 'em tender! Tracy and Fender!

AMBER is furious and horrified. She shoves BRENT away as if it were his fault. PENNY wildly applauds a beaming TRACY and FENDER.

CORNY
Tracy Turnblad, you're queen of the hop tonight. We're having auditions tomorrow for the Council. You ought to come on down and strut your stuff.

A stunned AMBER can't believe her ears.

TRACY
Oh, Corny, do you think I'm good enough?

CORNY
What d'ya think, kids?

TEENS applaud enthusiastically.

CORNY
(Continuing)
I hear ya! Thanks for comin', Tracy! See you tomorrow.

TRACY happily exits.

CORNY
(Continuing)
Well, Motormouth, it's time to slow things down a little with Mr. Gene Pitney.

MOTORMOUTH
(Whispering theatrically)
You can't hide your face in this godforsakin' place, right here in your city, the "Town Without Pity."

COUPLES start slow dancing to "Town Without Pity." A CREEP asks PENNY. We see LINK and AMBER clutching each other. AMBER is crying. FENDER and TRACY join the other COUPLES on dance floor. FENDER dances very closely, grinding. AMBER and LINK dance by with AMBER facing TRACY.

AMBER
(Mouthing the word hatefully)
Whore!

Tracy's back goes up, but before she can answer, LINK does a turn and is facing her. Tracy goes from anger to flirtation and mouths "hi." LINK winks and dances away. FENDER is mashing TRACY. We see AMBER and LINK making out. Other COUPLES follow suit and entire dance turns into giant make-out party. Even PENNY is kissed by CREEP after removing "red hot fireball" from mouth.

28) Dissolve to Exterior parking lot. TRACY and FENDER are making out in souped-up early 1960s car. We still hear "Town Without Pity" in background. He vigorously tries to get under Tracy's blouse, but she keeps pushing his hand away. We see dance breaking up, KIDS leaving. AMBER and LINK are walking through parking lot, giving out campaign fliers. They see TRACY getting huge passion mark from FENDER. AMBER looks scandalized but TRACY, noticing them, pulls away from FENDER

and smiles at LINK who smiles back. Suddenly a gang of TOUGHS pull
up in hot rod and yell insults out driver's-side windows.

> TOUGH A
>
> Well, look at the Corny Crabbers. The biggest assholes in town!

> TOUGH B
>
> Link, the dancin' fruit and tilted tits Amber, herself!

TRACY looks pissed. She shoves off FENDER and grabs a large can of
hairspray from her oversized pocketbook.

> LINK
> (Wearily)
> Step out of the car and say that!

Amber's been through this before and tries to pull Link away.

> LINK
> (Continuing)
> 'Cause my dancin' feet might feel like kickin' ass!

Out of nowhere, TRACY springs into action, spraying TOUGHS in face
with hairspray, temporarily blinding them. Car lurches away with
TOUGHS crying and cursing. TRACY winks at a stunned LINK who
laughs out loud and gives her a thumbs-up sign. AMBER, in a snit, drags
him away. FENDER is fumbling with his clothes, still panting.

29) Exterior other end of parking lot. PENNY is alone calling out for
TRACY. TRACY hears and rushes to her.

> PENNY
>
> Tracy, I had such a good time. It's *worth* being punished.

> TRACY
>
> I know, Penny. How much happiness can one girl take? I was in a
> gang fight, I've got a crush on Link, Corny asked me to audition,
> and Fender, a real-live Council Member, actually gave me a hickey.
> (Promptly showing it off)
> Isn't it a beauty? He almost sucked the skin right off my neck.
> (Happily)
> It *was* bleeding.

PENNY

Tracy, did you . . . you know . . . give?

TRACY

No, Penny, I'm not that kind of girl. I *did* let him dry-hump my leg briefly . . . the poor boy. Suppose he has blue balls?

Fade out.

30) Fade into Exterior Patterson Park High School. KIDS are entering, getting off school bus. We see PENNY with her "P" blouse. LINK and AMBER pull up in her sports car.

31) Exterior Eastern Avenue, main thoroughfare of Highlandtown. TRACY is in phone booth, dialing.

TRACY
(Disguising her voice)

Yes, this is Mrs. Edna Turnblad. I'm calling to say Tracy won't be in school today; she has the croup. The vaporizer has been on all night . . .

32) Interior high school homeroom. Before teacher arrives. AMBER is surrounded by adoring fans.

AMBER

. . . and anyway, she was right in the car in plain sight of just everybody at the hop! She was nude!

GIRL A

No?!

GIRL B

That fat thing?

AMBER

Tracy Turnblad is a whore!

33) Exterior Etta Gown shop, coolest teenage dress shop for East Baltimore girls. TRACY enters.

34) Interior Etta Gown Shop. HAIR-HOPPERS are shopping. A FEMALE TEENAGER models a bridal gown for her MOTHER. Hardboiled SALESLADY approaches TRACY.

> SALESLADY
> Can I help you?

> TRACY
> *(Handing her a gift certificate)*
> Yes, I won a Corny Collins dance contest.

> SALESLADY
> *(Eyeing her rudely)*
> We don't have nothin' in your size, hon.

As SALESLADY walks away, TRACY defiantly shoplifts one shoe off display counter.

35) Interior school lunchroom. AMBER is again surrounded, routinely signing autographs.

> AMBER
> . . . a gang bang! I saw it with my own eyes.

> GIRL B
> But is she a good dancer? That's what I want to know.

> AMBER
> She dances like what she is . . . a nymphomaniac!!

36) Exterior East Baltimore side street. The instrumental "Train to Nowhere" by the Champs is heard on the soundtrack. TRACY is prowling the streets looking for a place to lie low. She tries locked garage doors; DOGS bark, SNOOPY OLD LADIES eye her suspiciously. Finally, she sees Amber's parents, FRANKLIN and VELMA, leaving home, hiding front door key behind shutter and getting in fancy car. Tracy's eyes light up. She waits for them to leave, runs to the key, looks over her shoulder, and lets herself in.

37) *Interior Von Tussle home. TRACY nervously sneaks into Amber's bedroom. She goes through Amber's record collection, selects a 45, and plays it. We hear "Hey Baby" by Bruce Channel and see TRACY sloppily mixing Ultra Blue, a hair dye formula. TRACY applies the bleach and begins snooping in Amber's drawers and closet, reading her diary and making a big mess.*

38) *Interior classroom. AMBER sneakily passes a note. SHELLY opens it and we read "She's adopted."*

39) *Interior Amber's bedroom. TRACY styles her new bleach-blond hair, teasing it into giant bouffant. She applies Cleopatra eye makeup and covers her passion mark with heavy liquid makeup. Getting dressed in a more "fashionable" outfit and still wearing only one stolen shoe, she blows kisses to herself in mirror, mouths "thank you, thank you" like a star on "The Corny Collins Show," and exits.*

40) *Exterior School parking lot. AMBER is walking to car with LINK.*

                    AMBER
I've heard she even has mononucleosis!!

LINK rolls his eyeballs.

41) *Dissolve to Interior Etta Gown shop. We see SALESLADY muttering to herself as she replaces stolen shoe with its mate. We see TRACY spying through window. When SALESLADY goes into storeroom, TRACY runs in, swipes other shoe, puts it on her foot and runs out.*

42) *Wipe to Interior WZZT TV studio. PENNY, TRACY, and NADINE, a black teen girl, do "The New Continental," an even more complicated line dance than "The Madison." TAMMY is running the audition. We see CORNY to one side, watching, and AMBER, LINK, LOU ANN, BRAD, IQ, FENDER, SHELLY, SHANNON, CARMELITA, and CONSUELLA sitting at long table, furiously taking notes.*

                    TAMMY
              (Lifting needle of record)
Thank you girls. Now it's time to move on to a little something we call the "Spotlight." Okay. First girl, Miss Pingleton.

Poor PENNY *walks to center stage, nervously sucking her fireball as blinding light is shined on her. IQ aims mock TV camera at her.*

> PENNY
> *(Taking out fireball)*
> I'm just a little nervous.

> TAMMY
> This is show business, young lady! If you think you're nervous now, HA! Wait 'til you're on the air! Okay, first question!

COUNCIL MEMBERS approach PENNY one by one, firing questions.

> AMBER
> Are you now, or have you ever gone steady?

> PENNY
> Well . . . I'm not going with anybody now, but I'd love to date a Council Member.

COUNCIL MEMBERS shake their heads judgmentally and jot down notes.

> LOU ANN
> Exactly how many sweaters do you have?

> PENNY
> Gee, I've never counted. I guess about five.

We see COUNCIL mouth "five???" in disbelief and laugh.

> TAMMY
> Next!

PENNY sits down hurriedly, about to burst into tears. NADINE approaches "Spotlight."

> TAMMY
> *(Reading from notes)*
> Nadine Carver, Eastern High School.

DASH
You're aware Negro Day is the last Thursday of each month?

NADINE
Yes, I've been on it a few times, but I feel the show should be integrated. Every day.

IQ
Can you relate to Leslie Gore's music?

NADINE
(Losing patience)
Look, she ain't no James Brown, but I can dance to Lawrence Welk if I have to.

TAMMY
Thank you, Nadine.
(Reading)
Tracy Turnblad.

TRACY smiles at NADINE who scowls back, then excitedly takes "Spotlight."

BOBBY
Would you do a pimple cream commercial on camera if Corny asked you?

TRACY
I'd be proud to. Luckily, I've never been cursed with acne like others . . .
(Smiling at AMBER, who impulsively feels spot where pimple was)
. . . but I realize the devastating effect of skin blemishes on the social life of teenagers.

IQ
Would you ever . . .
(Distastefully)
. . . swim in an integrated swimming pool?

CORNY looks angry at the question.

TRACY

I certainly would, IQ! I'm a modern kind of gal. I'm all for integration.

CORNY *nods approvingly at Tracy's answer. We see AMBER fuming, losing her cool.*

AMBER

Aren't you a little FAT for the show?

TAMMY

That's enough, Amber!

TRACY

I would imagine that many of the home viewers are also . . . chunky . . . pleasingly plump.

AMBER

Oh, come on! The show's not in CinemaScope!

CORNY

You are out of line, Amber!

AMBER
(In a fit)
Corny, Tammy, can't you see? This girl is a trash can!

CORNY
(Jumping up)
That's five demerits, Amber. You are suspended from the show today! Pack up your things and go home!

AMBER
(Sobbing)
But Corny . . . I'm supposed to lead the Ladies' Choice!!

CORNY

I'm sure we can find a replacement!

AMBER
(Weakly)
Yes, Corny.

AMBER exits, whimpering.

TAMMY
(To the applicants)
Please wait outside. The Council will now meet in secret, debate
your personality flaws, and come to a final decision.

43) Wipe to Exterior Turnblad house. PENNY is banging on door. EDNA
answers.

EDNA
Penny Pingleton, you'll wake the dead! Tracy's not home yet. Plus,
your mother is on the warpath!

PENNY
I know, Miss Edna. Can I come in? There's something you both
gotta see!

EDNA
Well, come on in, but I got ironing, and Wilbur's working.

PENNY
(Turning and yelling—loudly)
MR. TURNBLAD!!!

44) Interior Turnblad's rec room. PENNY drags MISS EDNA to TV and
flicks it on.

EDNA
(Worried)
It's not war with Cuba is it? Or more Negro problems!!

PENNY
No, you'll see.

EDNA

Did poor Debbie Reynolds have a nervous breakdown? This better be good. Broad daylight and I'm sitting in front of a TV.

"The Corny Collins Show" comes on air. We see TRINKLETTES, black, all-girl group standing with CORNY, being interviewed.

EDNA
(Continuing)
I've *seen* "The Corny Collins Show," thank you Penny.

PENNY

Just watch!

WILBUR
(Entering)
I just lost a $2.69 Silly Putty sale. This better be worth it!

PENNY
Wait! You'll see. Just watch.

CORNY
(On TV)
Tell us where you're appearing tonight, girls.

GIRL A
We'll be at the Royal Theater . . .

GIRL B
In Motormouth Maybelle's . . .

GIRL C
All Soul Review!!

CORNY
Ladies and gentlemen, a big hand for Baltimore's own "TRINK-LETTES."

WILBUR
I closed up shop for this?!

CORNY

Let's keep the music playing and the hits a-turning with MR. GENE CHANDLER! The Duke of Earl loves to cha-cha-cha!

On TV, KIDS start doing the cha-cha as the "Duke of Earl" plays. We see TRACY on camera.

PENNY
(Proudly)
There! Look! It's Tracy!

EDNA
(Moving in closer)
Oh, my God! She's all peroxided up!

WILBUR
(Amazed)
Well, I'll be damned! Tracy's on TV.

EDNA
With a "triple process" yet!

PENNY
Tracy was accepted on the Corny Collins Council. Mr. and Mrs. Turnblad, your daughter is a star!

45) Cut to Interior Von Tussle home. FRANKLIN has AMBER across his knee, spanking her. VELMA sternly looks on. AMBER is yelping.

AMBER
Daddy! I *didn't* make a hairdo mess!

FRANKLIN
Add another spank for lying.

FRANKLIN wallops her.

VELMA
This isn't the Eldorado Beauty Academy! It's your home!

AMBER
I swear to God, I didn't do it!

FRANKLIN
(Spanking)
Liar! Liar! Liar! Liar!

46) *Interior TV studio. TRACY is cha-cha-chaing with FENDER. Camera with red "on-air" light blinking moves in and TRACY plays it for all its worth.*

47) *Interior Turnblad's rec room. Cut to Tracy's image on TV screen.*

PENNY
See?! She's already getting closeups!

EDNA
(In shock)
Does she get paid for this?
(Looking at Tracy's image on TV)
Big as a house!

WILBUR
I think she looks pretty, Edna.

Phone rings.

EDNA
(Answering)
Hello . . . why . . . yes . . . yes . . . I'm watching her now . . . You are? . . . Well, thank you . . . yes . . . goodbye.
(Hanging up)
That was Hilda from up Conkling Street. She's going to send a telegram!

48) *Interior Von Tussle's living room. AMBER is released from her spanking.*

FRANKLIN
Now, you may watch "The Corny Collins Show"!

AMBER, drying her tears, runs and turns on TV. She sees TRACY ending the cha-cha number.

AMBER

Oh, God! There she is!

49) Interior TV Studio. Cha-cha has ended. CORNY approaches TRACY.

CORNY

Now it's time to introduce somebody really special. A brand-new Council Member making her first appearance on the show today. And we *already* have telegrams. Why don't you introduce yourself?

TRACY

Hi, Corny. My name is Tracy Turnblad, and I go to Patterson Park.

Ladies' Choice—Link Larkin (Michael St. Gerard).

CORNY

Well, somebody out there likes you, Tracy.
(Reading)
"Please have the new girl lead a Ladies' Choice." Tell me, Tracy, are you going steady?

50) Interior Von Tussle's living room.

AMBER

I was supposed to lead the Ladies' Choice!!

51) Interior Turnblad's rec room.

TRACY
(On TV screen)
No, Corny, but there is somebody I've got a crush on . . .

BOYS on show line up in stag line. FENDER beams, thinking she means him.

EDNA

Who? I'd like to know! She's just a child.

PENNY
(Waving to screen)
Hi, Tracy. It's me, Penny!

EDNA
(To Penny)
She can't hear you.

52) Interior TV studio.

CORNY

Well, let's see who the lucky guy is. Ladies and gentlemen, a ladies' choice.

"You'll Lose a Good Thing" by Barbara Lynn plays as TRACY hesitates before stag line.

53) Interior Von Tussle's living room.

AMBER
She better hadn't dare!!!

54) Interior TV studio. TRACY moves towards FENDER, stops, changes her mind, smiles, puts out her hand, grabs LINK, and leads him to dance floor. FENDER is furious.

55) Interior Von Tussle's living room.

AMBER
(Jumping up, horrified, throwing ring down)
Oh God! He's violated the oath of the friendship ring!

AMBER goes into sobbing hysterics as PARENTS rush to comfort her.

56) Interior TV studio. Shot of LINK and TRACY dancing closely. CAMERAMAN seems to love them, moving in for closeups.

57) Interior Von Tussle's living room. As other COUPLES join in dancing on TV screen, FRANKLIN flicks off TV.

FRANKLIN
Don't cry, honey.

VELMA
That fat girl's no competition! You could tell her hair wasn't even done professionally.

FRANKLIN
White trash! Plain and simple!

VELMA
For all we know, that girl could be high yellow.

AMBER
(Sobbing)
Mummy . . . daddy . . . I'll still be the Queen of the Auto Show, won't I?

58) Exterior TV studio. TRACY and LINK are mobbed by new FANS. TRACY signs autographs, thrilled.

59) Interior Turnblad's rec room. EDNA hangs up phone and it rings again . . . immediately.

> EDNA
>
> Hello . . . no, she's not here. Well, I'm sure she loves you, too. Thank you.
> *(Hanging up)*
> This is amazing.

> PENNY
>
> She's so popular already!

> EDNA
> *(Hopefully)*
> She could be one of the June Taylor Dancers . . .

Phone rings.

> EDNA
> *(Continuing)*
> Hello . . . No, she's not here. Well . . . thank you. I know she'll appreciate your vote.
> *(Hanging up, amazed)*
> . . . or even *Miss Auto Show.*

> PENNY
>
> She's gonna win, I can feel it!

> WILBUR
>
> Maybe we'll be rich!

> EDNA
>
> I won't have to take in ironing!

Phone rings, EDNA snatches it off receiver.

> EDNA
> *(Continuing)*
> Hello . . . Well . . . Yes . . . *I* am Tracy Turnblad's agent, how can I help you?

EDNA grabs pencil and jots down information. TRACY rushes in.
WILBUR and PENNY run to her applauding.

> PENNY
> Oh, Tracy, you were wonderful!

> WILBUR
> We're real proud of you, honey.

> EDNA
> *(Hanging up phone and running to embrace TRACY)*
> Tomorrow try and get up a little closer so we can see you better.

> WILBUR
> Maybe even give the "Hardy-Har" a little plug . . .

> TRACY
> Oh, Mom, oh, Dad, oh, Penny—my best friend. I'm so happy.
> Finally, all of Baltimore knows—I'm big, blonde, and beautiful!

> PENNY
> You're a teen leader now!

> EDNA
> And the show-biz offers are pouring in! We've got an audition
> tonight and honey, it's only the beginning! Stick with me, baby, and
> we'll claw our way to the top!

> TRACY
> *(Beside herself with teen joy)*
> Oh, God! Fame! Glamour! Fortune! And to top it all off . . . I'M
> IN LOVE!!!

60) Fade in to Exterior Eastern Avenue. Night. "Mama Didn't Lie" by Jan
Bradley is heard on soundtrack. We see an embarrassed TRACY walking
with EDNA, who insists on holding her hand. TEENS recognize TRACY
and ask for autographs. EDNA is proud. A transit bus pulls up and
BLACK TEEN leans head out window and yells, "Tracy, you are really
baaaad!" EDNA looks nervous and yanks her away. They approach exte-
rior of Hefty Hideaway, a specialty clothing store for overweight women,
pause, and enter.

61) Interior Hefty Hideaway. HUGE CUSTOMERS are shopping, trying on clothes, admiring themselves in mirror and snacking from trays of brownies and candies that are placed throughout store. MR. PINKY, a hillbilly hair-hopper, bejeweled with pinky rings, is fitting a HUGE CUSTOMER.

                    MR. PINKY
You look gorgeous, Bertha. Simply exquisite!

HUGE CUSTOMER looks unsure.

                    MR. PINKY
                 (Continuing)
Care for an éclair?
                 (Seeing TRACY and EDNA and jumping up)
TRACY TURNBLAD! Welcome to the Hefty Hideaway, house of fashion for the ample woman! I'm Mr. Pinky!

                    TRACY
                 (Nervously)
Hi.

Ricki and Divine after makeover.

EDNA

Mr. Pinky, I'm Tracy's . . . business manager, Edna Turnblad.

MR. PINKY

It's a pleasure to meet you both.
(To TRACY)
Here we cater to the big-boned girls like yourself who are stylish,
and at the same time frustrated by the lack of sizes in the department
stores today. I saw you on TV and I'd like you to be my model!

*HUGE CUSTOMERS are trying on ludicrous, early 1960s fashions and
admiring themselves in mirrors throughout rest of the scene.*

EDNA

Would . . . would she be paid?

MR. PINKY

One free outfit a month.
(To TRACY)
You start tomorrow! And, let's hope there are no diets in the works,
because I want to design your Miss Auto Show coronation gown
myself!

EDNA

Could . . . could we include some complimentary petty pants in
the deal?

MR. PINKY

You drive a hard bargain, Miss Edna, and rightfully so. Petty pants?
Panty girdle? Let Tracy take her pick!

EDNA

(Aggressively)
How about a fabulous frock just for me?

MR. PINKY

Tracy will have to work one extra day for free.

EDNA

It's a deal!
(Thrilled)
Thank you, Mr. Pinky.

62) *Dissolve to Exterior Eastern Avenue night. TRACY and EDNA are walking up "The Avenue" in outrageously colorful, new, stylish outfits. We hear "Train to Nowhere" by the Champs once again on soundtrack. TRACY stops in front of Eldorado Beauty Academy and drags EDNA in. Jump cut to EDNA leaving with new hairdo—giant "barrel curls." TRACY is beaming. Music fades out and TRACY turns to EDNA.*

> TRACY
> *(Proudly)*
> Momma . . . welcome to the sixties!!

63) *Dissolve to Interior high school. Next day. TRACY is reading* HairDo *magazine as TEACHER drones on in Geometry class. BOY STUDENT behind her in vainly trying to pay attention but struggles to see blackboard blocked by Tracy's giant hairdo. TEACHER notices.*

> TEACHER
> What *is* the problem, Mr. Davis?

> BOY STUDENT
> I can't see through her hair!

> TRACY
> I can't help it if he's short.

> TEACHER
> Your ratted hair is preventing yet another student's Geometry education . . .

> TRACY
> It's "feathered," not ratted.

> TEACHER
> Whatever you call it, it's a hair-don't. And you've been warned repeatedly.
> *(Scribbling a note)*
> I want you to take a little walk down to the principal's office. We'll see what he has to say!

64) Interior Principal's office waiting room. TRACY enters and we see a weeping GIRL, being dragged out and smacked by her ANGRY MOTHER. TRACY gulps. MR. DAVIDSON, stern principal, leans head out door of his office.

MR. DAVIDSON
Tracy?

TRACY gets up, fixes her hair, and goes in.

65) Interior Principal's office.

MR. DAVIDSON
Have a seat . . .

TRACY
Yes, sir.

MR. DAVIDSON
Once again your hairdo is getting you in hot water. Didn't two weeks in Hairdo Detention have any effect?

TRACY
(Snippily)
I happen to be the height of teen fashion!

MR. DAVIDSON
You're on a one-way ticket to reform school. I'm afraid I'm going to have to change your homeroom. Starting today, I want you to report to Class 10-D, Room 78.

TRACY
(Horrified)
Special Ed?

MR. DAVIDSON
Yes, Miss Turnblad. Special Education.

TRACY
But . . . that's for retards!
(Defiantly)
And the smart black kids you try to hold back.

51

MR. DAVIDSON
Here you will be taught by specialists trained in dealing with hairdo scofflaws in high school society . . .

TRACY
But, Mr. Davidson . . .

MR. DAVIDSON
That will be all, Miss Turnblad. You may go now . . .

TRACY *angrily gets up to leave.*

MR. DAVIDSON
(Continuing)
Oh, yes, one more thing.

TRACY *glares at him.*

MR. DAVIDSON
(Continuing)
Have you taken a good, hard look in the mirror lately?

MR. DAVIDSON *holds up a large hand-mirror that catches her framed reflection perfectly.*

MR. DAVIDSON
(Continuing)
I would advise it, Miss Turnblad. You look like an utter fool!

MR. DAVIDSON *laughs obnoxiously in her face.* TRACY *slams door angrily and exits.*

66) *Interior Special Ed class. STUDENTS are hanging out in a small class-room. Many are black. Another student is a RETARDED-LOOKING WHITE GIRL. A TRAMPY HILLBILLY GIRL with missing teeth and a monstrous, home-done beehive hairdo decorated with plastic bumblebees, lets a SLOW LEARNER feel her bra straps. TRACY enters; some of the KIDS recognize her and applaud. SEAWEED, a handsome black kid, is dancing with himself and humming hit tunes. TRACY smiles at him. Suddenly, MISS SHIPLEY, the Special Ed teacher, enters and STUDENTS jump into their seats and quiet down.*

MISS SHIPLEY

Good morning, Class.

ALL

Good morning, Miss Shipley.

MISS SHIPLEY

You may have noticed we have a new student joining Special Education today.
(To TRACY)
Stand and introduce yourself.

TRACY

I'm Tracy Turnblad . . .
(Throwing caution to the wind)
TV star! Model! And future Miss Auto Show 1962!

Class applauds wildly.

MISS SHIPLEY

(To Class)
Welcome to Special Education, Tracy, where teen problems become a thing of the past. Now, let's all stand for the Pledge of Allegiance and the Lord's Prayer.

ALL stand and place hands over hearts. As they recite Pledge, SEAWEED smiles at TRACY and does first hand-step of the "Hand Jive." CLASS MEMBERS join in routine of "Hand Jive." As the Lord's Prayer begins, entire CLASS is doing it behind Miss Shipley's back. As Prayer ends, she turns around. The whole CLASS stops "Hand Jive" and feigns respect.

MISS SHIPLEY

(Continuing)
Now, as we all know, this morning is Special Ed's turn in the Dodge Ball Tournament! So, let's go to the locker room, change into our gym outfits, and show them that Special Ed is nothing to laugh about!

TRACY almost collapses.

67) Exterior gym field. HOMEROOM 10-C is already waiting, dressed in gym suits, tossing ball back and forth. We see PENNY in crowd. AMBER and LINK are fighting.

> LINK
> *(To AMBER)*
> Come on, Amber! Can't we just be friends?

AMBER turns her back to him, refusing to speak.

Suddenly, pitiful SPECIAL ED team runs out of gym to hoots from HOMEROOM 10-C. We see TRACY, extremely embarrassed to be seen in gym outfit. AMBER spots her and laughs cruelly. SEAWEED catches up to TRACY and accompanies her to game. AMBER runs off in a huff to GYM TEACHER who flips coin and AMBER calls it.

> GYM TEACHER
> Special Ed in the ring!

Dodge Ball game begins. HOMEROOM 10-C forms a large circle and SPECIAL ED gets in middle. Object of game is to be the last person hit by the ball. When you are hit, you leave the inner circle. If you catch the ball, you are safe. HOMEROOM 10-C aims and hurls the ball at terrified SPECIAL ED team in middle who keep scrambling to other side of circle. TRACY is petrified. SEAWEED catches the ball several times before it hits TRACY. As game is played, TRACY tries to talk to PENNY and LINK who are on outside of the ring. Entire dialog is spoken as frantic game takes place.

> TRACY
> *(Hurriedly)*
> Penny, they put me in Special Ed! Just 'cause of my hair!

TRACY runs from ball.

> LINK
> *(Beckoning)*
> Tracy!! Over here. Wanna ride the bus with me to the show? I've got an extra transfer.

> TRACY
> *(Running to LINK)*

I'd love to.

> *(Embarrassed)*

But, please, Link . . . don't look at my legs without the benefit of nylons . . .

TRACY runs away.

> AMBER

GET THE FAT ONE!

AMBER throws ball at TRACY, but misses.

> SEAWEED
> *(To TRACY)*

Hey, I saw you on "The Corny Collins Show." Where'd a white girl learn to dance like that?

> TRACY

Just practicing.
> *(Bashful)*

And watching "Negro Day" on Corny Collins.

> AMBER
> *(To TRACY)*

Hey, Thunder Thighs! This one's for you!

> SEAWEED
> *(Catching ball to not be eliminated)*

My mother says Negro Day is nothing but segregation.

> TRACY
> *(Watching for ball, terrified)*

Your mother?

> SEAWEED

None other than Motormouth Maybelle, herself!

TRACY
(Running to PENNY in outside circle)
See the colored boy? The cute one? His mother is Motormouth
Maybelle!

PENNY
(Blushing)
He's gorgeous.

There are only about three left in the circle. CROWD is going wild.
AMBER is furious. TRACY is being protected.

AMBER
Tracy! This ball's gonna *sting* when it hits!

TRACY
You mess up my hair, and I'll kick your ass!

LINK is impressed. AMBER throws ball. SEAWEED tries to catch it but
misses and is eliminated.

SEAWEED
(To TRACY)
Sorry, I tried. Hey, stop by my mom's record shop after the show.
It's right off North Avenue. We can BOOOOGEEEE!!!

SEAWEED leaves circle. Only TRACY and JOCK-TYPE are left in the ring.

AMBER
Get the fat retard!

AMBER throws ball as hard as she can and hits TRACY square in the
head. TRACY staggers around ring, stunned, before passing out cold with
a thud. GYM TEACHER blows whistle to end game. AMBER is laughing
and being congratulated. SEAWEED, PENNY, and LINK rush to Tracy's
prone body and try to revive her. Seaweed and Penny's eyes lock, and they
stare love-struck at one another as ridiculous, romantic music is heard on
soundtrack.

LINK kneels down over TRACY.

                    LINK
Come on girl . . . you're all right . . . it's not who wins, but how you
play the game . . .

TRACY *sees LINK in a blurry POV shot. He starts to come into focus as*
she regains consciousness.

                    LINK
                (Continuing)
Tracy . . . will you go steady with me?

TRACY *smiles foggily and happily accepts.*

68) *Interior TV studio.* "The Corny Collins Show" *is in full progress.*
LINK and TRACY are wildly twisting to Chubby Checker's "Let's Twist
Again," TRACY theatrically making sure the camera sees her new friend-
ship ring.

69) *Interior Turnblad's rec room. EDNA and WILBUR are watching and*
doing a lame version of the Twist. PENNY jumps on sofa and twists
wildly, showing them how to do it. EDNA and WILBUR start gyrating in
a frenzy of parental pride.

On the air.

70) *Interior TV studio. AMBER is twisting with FENDER, fuming and glaring at TRACY and LINK. TAMMY signals to TRACY on dance floor with "Hefty Hideaway" cue card and TRACY twists off dance floor with LINK. AMBER is twisting wildly when camera approaches, butting in front of FENDER for better coverage. Dance ends and KIDS applaud.*

TRACY begins modeling tacky 1960s outfit on amateurish, mock-up set, as MR. PINKY stands in front with microphone giving his sales pitch.

MR. PINKY
(In a sing-song voice)

Fatty! Fatty! 2 by 4—couldn't get through the dressing room door! Hi. I'm Mr. Pinky, owner of the Hefty Hideaway, 3201 Eastern Avenue. Are you big-boned? Got a glandular problem, but still want glamour?

(Pointing to TRACY as she models)

The Hefty Hideaway's got it all! This beautiful two-piece ensemble modeled by our lovely Tracy, is available in sizes 12–26! We've got girdles! Even large-sized shoes for that continental Clementine look! All at prices you can afford . . .

71) *Interior Turnblad's rec room. EDNA, WILBUR, and PENNY are watching proudly.*

WILBUR
(Wiping away a tear)

That's our little baby . . .

EDNA
(Taking a photo of TV screen)

She's prettier than Elizabeth Taylor . . .

PENNY

Eat your heart out, Annette Funicello!

72) *Interior TV studio. AMBER watches MR. PINKY disgustedly.*

MR. PINKY

The Hefty Hideaway! Come in today! You'll be glad you did!

CORNY walks on camera.

CORNY

Thank you, Mr. Pinky. We're thrilled to have you as a new sponsor. And Tracy, keep this up, and you might be crowned Miss Auto Show 1962!!

AMBER *fumes hatefully.*

73) Interior Turnblad's rec room. WILBUR, EDNA, and PENNY are wildly cheering.

CORNY
(On TV screen)
. . . that's it for today, kids, but remember, tomorrow is Pre-Teen Day. So, bring your little brother . . .

Doorbell rings.

PENNY
Oh, God, it's probably my mother!

CORNY
. . . your little sister, and let those tykes rock 'n' roll on . . .

EVERYBODY ON TV and WILBUR and EDNA
THE CORNY COLLINS SHOW!!!

EDNA flicks off TV and goes to answer door.

EDNA
(Answering)
Good afternoon, Prudy. Have you been watching the show? My daughter Tracy . . .

MRS. PINGLETON
(Rushing to daughter)
Come here, you!

PENNY is jumping over furniture to get away.

PENNY

Stop following me, you witch!

WILBUR

Would you care for a Yoo-Hoo, Prudy?

MRS. PINGLETON

You're punished for the rest of your life.

EDNA

Maybe if you sat down together and had a heart to heart, mother-daughter talk . . .

PENNY bolts for the door, and she runs away. WILBUR and EDNA are stunned.

MRS. PINGLETON
(Yelling out window)

Penny Pingleton! IF YOU EVER HAVE CHILDREN, THEY'RE PUNISHED TOO!
(The ultimate threat)
I'M TELLING YOUR FATHER!

MRS. PINGLETON runs after PENNY.

74) *Interior moving transit bus. TRACY and LINK are mobbed by TEEN RIDERS. As they pass Hefty Hideaway, we see mob of FAT GIRLS entering or leaving with packages. As bus pulls to stop, TRACY waves out window and FAT GIRLS go wild at seeing their idol. Suddenly, we see PENNY running up the street calling to TRACY as MRS. PINGLETON chases her daughter in hot pursuit. PENNY barely makes it on to the bus before her mother can grab her. The bus pulls off and PENNY happily joins LINK and TRACY.*

75) *Exterior Eastern Avenue. A frantic MRS. PINGLETON hails a taxi and follows the bus.*

76) *Exterior street corner in West Baltimore neighborhood. TRACY, PENNY, and LINK get off bus, looking slightly intimidated but excited by all the black faces, and proceed up the street.*

77) Exterior West Baltimore street. MRS. PINGLETON, in taxicab, spots TRACY, PENNY, and LINK just as they go around corner. MRS. PINGLETON gets out of cab, pays the driver, and looks around in terror at being alone in this part of town.

78) Interior Motormouth Maybelle's Record Store. "The Bird" by the Five Du-Tones is playing and BLACK TEENAGERS, dressed in style of early 1960s, are doing the dance, which consists of various steps of flapping your arms. We see SEAWEED dancing with his sister, L'IL INEZ, who is about ten years old, wears a starched, frilly "party dress," and is a great dancer. We also see NADINE, the black girl who was earlier rejected from the Council, "birding" away with PARTNER. MOTORMOUTH is behind counter, spinning the records, ringing up sales, and sometimes dancing in place.

TRACY, LINK, and PENNY enter. MOTORMOUTH sees them first and waves, as they shyly watch the dancing. Gradually, OTHERS see them and whisper while dancing. Finally, L'IL INEZ spots them and rushes over.

> L'IL INEZ
Tracy Turnblad! You're my favorite dancer on Corny Collins! I'm L'il Inez, Seaweed's sister.

> TRACY
It's nice to meet you, L'il Inez. This is my best friend Penny, and Link you probably know from the show.

> SEAWEED
> *(Coming over)*
Wow! You really came! Everyone, this is Tracy, the baddest white dancer in town! Hey, Ma, play that record again!

> MOTORMOUTH
Hey, whatever you heard, it's time to teach the white children "The Bird"!

MOTORMOUTH starts playing "The Bird" again and the tension is broken. BLACK TEENAGERS start flapping. SEAWEED grabs PENNY as a partner and drags her out. LINK and TRACY go on dance floor and start trying to do "The Bird."

79) *Exterior West Baltimore ghetto street. MRS. PINGLETON is terrified. Two OLD BLACK LADIES cackle when they see her ridiculous paranoia. OLD BLACK WINO approaches.*

> WINO
> *(Drukenly)*
> Miss White Lady, could you spare a quarter so I could get me some wine to aid my discomfort?

> MRS. PINGLETON
> Oh, God, somebody PLEASE HELP ME!

BLACKS on street burst out laughing.

> MRS. PINGLETON
> *(Taking out wallet in a panic)*
> Here, take it all! But please don't hurt me!! PLEEEASE!! PLEEEASE!!

> WINO
> *(Taking a dollar out of her wallet)*
> Why thank you, ma'am!!

MRS. PINGLETON runs in a panic as BLACKS howl in laughter.

80) *Interior Record Shop. All the KIDS are wildly doing "The Bird." L'IL INEZ is dancing with TRACY and LINK. PENNY, love-struck, is flapping away with SEAWEED. Even MOTORMOUTH is flapping behind counter. NADINE flaps aggressively to TRACY and LINK, then to SEAWEED and PENNY. NADINE is the only unfriendly face and makes it known she resents the new arrivals. SEAWEED tries to humor NADINE, but she gives him a dirty look and "birds" away. Song ends and EVERYONE applauds.*

> TRACY
> Now *I've* got a dance to show you. We're forbidden to do it on "The Corny Collins Show" . . .

> PENNY
> Oh, Tracy, do we dare?

LINK

You mean the "Dirty Boogie"?

TRACY

Yes I do! Motormouth, do you have the record "Hide and Seek"?

MOTORMOUTH

I ain't no pill, it's Bunker Hill. Won't be long, I introduced that song!

TRACY

Play it loud! All the white kids are doin' this dance and it's NAAASTY!

Record plays and TRACY, PENNY, and LINK start demonstrating the mildly obscene "Dirty Boogie," a bumping and grinding dance with improvisational, suggestive arm movements. BLACK TEENAGERS howl in disbelief.

81) Exterior Record Store. MRS. PINGLETON runs down street in fear, hiding in alleyways, running at the sight of even a single black person. She runs by record store, hears music, and fearfully creeps to window and looks in. She sees PENNY and SEAWEED "obscenely" doing the "Dirty Boogie," along with all the other BLACK TEENAGERS. The color drains from Mrs. Pingleton's face, and she almost faints. We see a police car pull by and stop at light. MRS. PINGLETON approaches COP, he turns around and she sees he's black. She screams in terror and runs back toward record store in hysterics. COP laughs in astonishment.

82) Interior Record Store. EVERYBODY is doing "Dirty Boogie," even MOTORMOUTH MAYBELLE, who bumps and grinds with hilarious abandon. MRS. PINGLETON bursts in door and pulls out nail file for protection.

MRS. PINGLETON
(With ludicrous bravado)

Don't anybody come near me!! I'm armed and I'm prepared to pro-tect myself!

Everybody stops dancing, stunned.

                    PENNY
            (Supremely embarrassed)
Oh God, Mother!!

                MRS. PINGLETON
    (Poking nail file at anyone who gets near her)
I know you were snatched, Penny, and I've come to save you.

                MOTORMOUTH
Ooooh-pap-a-tunie! We got a loonie!

                MRS. PINGLETON
        (Turning on her with nail file)
Don't try your voodoo spells on me, native woman!

                    PENNY
We're *just* dancing!

                    TRACY
Mrs. Pingleton, these are our friends. Stop acting crazy!

                MRS. PINGLETON
            (Rushing to grab PENNY)
Don't act ignorant, Tracy Turnblad!
            (Dragging PENNY out)
Come on! Penny! Run! Run! Run for your life!

*All of the BLACK TEENAGERS howl in laughter as TRACY and LINK
shake their heads in disbelief. Fade out.*

*83) Fade in to Exterior WZZT the next day. Tracking shot of line of PRE-
TEENS waiting with PARENTS to get on show. PRE-TEENS are hilariously dressed in imitation of Council Members. We see LITTLE GIRLS
with giant bouffant hairdos and tight skirts. LITTLE BOYS are dressed
as little men in mock-suits and hats. PARENTS nag the PRE-TEENS to
fix their outfits. We see SEAWEED and PENNY accompanying L'IL
INEZ in the line. PENNY is reading* Black Like Me.

*84) Interior TV studio. Show in progress. PRE-TEENS are doing the gim-
mick dance "The Fly" by Chubby Checker. We see AMBER signing autographs surrounded by PRE-TEENS. We see VELMA wearing matching*

mother/daughter outfit, watching approvingly from sidelines, but her face turns to stone as she sees TRACY and LINK enter accompanied by EDNA, also dressed in matching mother/daughter outfit. PRE-TEENS leave AMBER and rush to TRACY and LINK.

85) Exterior TV studio. More PRE-TEENS and their PARENTS are being admitted. When SEAWEED, PENNY, and L'IL INEZ reach the door, a SECURITY OFFICER blocks their entrance.

> SECURITY GUARD
> *(Embarrassed)*
> I'm sorry, Pre-Teen Day is a white-only show. Next Thursday is Negro Day.

> SEAWEED
> You turning this little girl away?

> SECURITY GUARD
> I don't make the rules.

> SEAWEED
> Aren't you aware of the Supreme Court ruling on segregation?

> L'IL INEZ
> I have a dream!

> LADY A
> *(Behind her)*
> You heard the man. You're holding up the line.

> PENNY
> *(Yelling ridiculously)*
> SEGREGATION NEVER! INTEGRATION NOW!

86) Interior TV studio. CORNY is surrounded by adoring PRE-TEENS.

> CORNY
> Okay, you little tykes! We have a real treat in store! A local group with a big hit record! Let's have a warm welcome for the Lafayettes!

John Waters and the "pre-teen" guests.

PRE-TEENS applaud as the white group THE LAFAYETTES lip-synch their hit "Life's Too Short." While they sing, the lead singer, NICK, a handsome greaser, eyeballs AMBER who watches transfixed, flirting back. VELMA encourages her daughter, pushing her closer. We see the SECURITY GUARD approach CORNY off camera.

> SECURITY GUARD
>
> Mr. Collins, there's some trouble outside. There's a little black girl who wants to be on the show.

> CORNY
>
> Let her in, for God's sake.

> SECURITY GUARD
>
> The station management says "No." And she is with some agitators. I'm afraid a demonstration is in the works.

TRACY and LINK rush to the exit door. SECURITY GUARD blocks them and MISS EDNA tries to pull them back. VELMA watches disgustedly.

Mother/daughter outfits (Colleen Fitzpatrick, Debbie Harry, Divine, Ricki Lake).

EDNA
Tracy, don't get involved. You can't change the world in a day.

TRACY and LINK
(Yelling)
Two! Four! Six! Eight! TV's got to integrate!

87) Exterior TV studio. PENNY, SEAWEED, and L'IL INEZ are sitting in, refusing to budge, singing "We Shall Overcome." They see LINK and TRACY trying to get out, picking up their chant. A NEWS TEAM arrives.

88) Interior TV studio. THE LAFAYETTES are finishing song as AMBER flirts outrageously. CORNY goes on camera to applause.

CORNY

Let's have a hand for the long, tall, lanky Lafayettes. Now, kids, we're going to get *real* lovey-dovey. I know this is one of your favorite records, and it's one of mine, too. Leslie Gore, sing your heart out!

Leslie Gore's "You Don't Own Me," plays as TAMMY coaxes PRE-TEENS to slow-dance on camera. NICK asks AMBER to dance off camera and starts grinding suggestively, feeling Amber's ass. AMBER throws nose in air at LINK, trying to make him jealous. VELMA looks thrilled.

CORNY and TAMMY are arguing with MR. HODGEPILE, WZZT's owner.

CORNY
(Continuing)
What difference does it make? One little black girl?!

TAMMY
It's an easy way to integrate without trouble!
(Seeing AMBER and NICK)
Amber! That's five demerits!!

MR. HODGEPILE
Absolutely not! Baltimore is not ready for integrated dancing!

Shot of EDNA holding back TRACY and LINK who are still chanting and trying to leave studio. VELMA approaches haughtily.

VELMA
(To EDNA)
Can I ask you a personal question?

EDNA
(Still restraining KIDS; highly suspicious)
No, you can't.

VELMA
Is your daughter mulatto?

> EDNA
> *(Losing temper, letting go of KIDS to slap VELMA)*

Why . . . you . . . you . . .

TAMMY separates EDNA and VELMA as TRACY and LINK run from studio.

> EDNA
> *(Yelling after them)*

Tracy Turnblad, you're going to be in big trouble, honey, big trouble.

> *(In desperation)*

YOU DIDN'T EVEN OPEN YOUR FAN MAIL!!!

> *(To TAMMY, getting a hold of herself)*

Tammy, I've heard so much about you. I know this isn't the time or place, but is there any way the cameraman can favor Tracy's left profile? I mean, she's such a lovely child and . . .

> TAMMY
> *(Annoyed, throwing hands in air)*

Good Lord Almighty!!!

AMBER and NICK wildly make out as PRE-TEENS dance, pointing and giggling. TAMMY rushes over and yanks them apart. VELMA tries to push them back. TAMMY and CORNY can't believe their eyes. EDNA, still confused, looks on in disgust.

89) Exterior TV studio. TRACY, LINK, PENNY, SEAWEED, L'IL INEZ chant, "Two, four, six eight," as NEWS TEAM films them. A police car pulls up and the KIDS take off running.

90) Interior TV studio. CORNY is hastily closing the show, rattled.

> CORNY

That's it for today, kids. See you tomorrow—three o'clock. Live at Tilted Acres!!!!!

CORNY rushes off camera to TAMMY, who hands him a half pint of whiskey. He swigs and passes it to TAMMY who eagerly accepts.

Directing the "Coliseum" kids.

91) Exterior Coliseum Dance Hall. Night. BLACK TEENS, dressed in style of early 1960s, are pouring into a dance.

92) Interior Coliseum Dance Hall. "I'm Blue," by the Ikettes, is playing and all the BLACK TEENAGERS are dancing. We see, buried in the crowd, TRACY, LINK, PENNY, SEAWEED, and L'IL INEZ doing a torrid "Dirty Boogie." MOTORMOUTH enters to thunderous applause. L'IL INEZ and SEAWEED rush over and kiss her while LINK, PENNY, TRACY, and CROWD whistle and cheer. PENNY wipes away a tear of happiness and MOTORMOUTH takes the stage.

MOTORMOUTH

Black Baltimore! Your mother is ready to show her might and fight, fight, fight!! Ooh poppity lickit, we gotta pickit. There ain't no way, ain't no way, we gonna stand for Negro Day! Negro Day! Negro Day!

BLACK TEENAGERS applaud, scream, and cheer.

MOTORMOUTH
(Continuing)
After school, you know where to go, Tilted Acres for the show! Segregation. No! No! No!

BLACK TEENAGERS
(Chanting back militantly)
Segregation. No! No! No!

MOTORMOUTH
(Continuing)
And now I'd like to introduce my main man. I'm his biggest fan. All the way from Chattanooga, Tennessee, just to see big bad me. He's got the most soulful record on the chart and he's awful smart! Let's have a ball in the hall. He's a living doll! Mr. Toussaint McCall!

BLACK TEENAGERS applaud wildly.

TOUSSAINT McCALL*, a touchingly un-flashy soul singer, comes on stage. BLACK TEENAGE GIRLS in audience squeal in delight. L'IL INEZ is right up front. TOUSSAINT McCALL sings his incredibly moving signature song, "Nothing Takes the Place of You" as TEENS watch, transfixed. COUPLES start slow-dancing and making out.

We see LINK and TRACY and SEAWEED and PENNY dance in the heat of teenage, untamed passion. TOUSSAINT McCALL catches Penny's eye and blows her a kiss. SEAWEED, slightly jealous, dances PENNY to exit and out. LINK and TRACY follow.

93) Exterior trash-strewn back alley. RATS scurry about. A beautiful, full moon. Both COUPLES start making out. We still hear Toussaint McCall's "Nothing Takes the Place of You" playing in the background. We see OLD BLACK BUM walking down alley looking in trash cans. He hears music playing inside and starts singing along with "Nothing Takes the Place of You" in a beautiful voice. Both COUPLES watch him like they've seen a vision. He tips his hat to them, chuckles, and walks by.

TRACY
(Moved)
Oh, Link, this is so romantic.

*Playing himself.

A RAT nibbles Tracy's shoe and she kicks it away.

> TRACY
> *(Continuing)*
> I wish . . . I wish I was dark skinned.

> LINK
> *(Passionately)*
> Tracy, our *souls* are black, even though our skin is white.

> PENNY
> *(Moaning)*
> Seaweed . . . Seaweed . . . will integration ever come?

> SEAWEED
> *(Groaning)*
> Oh, Penny, my little white lily . . . we're outcasts from both societies . . . white . . . black . . . our love is taboo!

> PENNY
> *(Clutching his hand to her breast)*
> Go to second! Go to second!

A car with lights on high beams comes down alley. We see WILBUR behind the wheel and a concerned EDNA next to him. All sorts of "Hardy Har" dashboard decorations light up and move ridiculously.

> EDNA
> *(Calling out window)*
> Tracy! Tracy Turnblad! It's your mommy!

> WILBUR
> We're worried about you, honey! Please come home! We have a surprise!

> EDNA
> Penny, your mother is on her way WITH your father!

Headlights reveal hiding kids.

EDNA
(Continuing)

There they are!

WILBUR sounds car horn which has been rigged up with obnoxious honk. KIDS run. WILBUR and EDNA take chase in car. OLD BLACK BUM sees the whole thing and when EDNA and WILBUR pull to corner after losing the KIDS' trail, he signals EDNA and WILBUR in the wrong direction.

94) Exterior West Baltimore street. PENNY, SEAWEED, LINK, and TRACY race down street banging on doors of people's houses. NEIGHBORS peer out, slam doors in their faces. One door opens and way-out BEAT GIRL with long, straight hair, answers, as the KIDS see Turnblad car approaching in distance. BEAT GIRL grabs KIDS inside.

95) Interior grungy beatnik pad. In one corner is lunatic BEATNIK "CAT" wildly doing bad abstract paintings, flinging paint everywhere. The BEAT GIRL is really out of it. The KIDS look nervous but relieved to find a place to hide.

BEAT GIRL

Like, hi, cats. Is that the fuzz chasing you?

SEAWEED

No . . . we . . .

(Amazed)

Wow, real beatniks!!

LINK

Just like in New York!!

BEATNIK "CAT" totally ignores them, throwing paint in a frenzy.

BEAT GIRL
(Grabbing bongos and singing loudly)

DAY-O!!E-DA-DA-DA-E-DA-DA!!! Daylight comin' and he wanna go home!!!

(Back to "normal," to TRACY and PENNY)

You two checkerboard chicks?

PENNY
(Confused)
What?

BEAT GIRL
You know, black 'n' white? Salt and pepper?

PENNY
Well . . . yes. *I* am a checkerboard chick . . . I guess.

TRACY
(Boldly)
I'm an integrationist. We shall overcome someday.

BEAT GIRL
Not with *that* hair, you won't. You look like a hair-hopper to me.
Like, your hair is really uncool.

LINK
She happens to be a TV star.

BEAT GIRL
Oh, big deal!!

BEATNIK "CAT" starts growling and destroying painting, oblivious to "guests." BEAT GIRL ignores him. The KIDS are starting to get very uncomfortable.

TRACY
(Trying to make small talk)
How do you get your hair so straight and . . .
(repulsed)
. . . so *flat?*

BEAT GIRL
With an iron, man. I play my bongos, listen to Odetta, and then I
iron my hair. You dig?

> LINK
> *(Eyeing raving BEATNIK "CAT" nearby)*

We better be going.

> *(Looking out window)*

The coast is clear.

> SEAWEED
> *(Despairingly)*

I'm gonna get lynched.

> BEAT GIRL

Hey, let's do some reefer! We'll get high and I'll iron the chick's hair! Dig?

BEATNIK "CAT" takes entire canvas and pokes head through it violently.

> BEATNIK "CAT"
> *(Menacing at KIDS)*

REEEEEEFER!!

> PENNY
> *(Uptight)*

Reefer?

> SEAWEED
> *(Appalled)*

I think they mean marijuana.

> TRACY
> *(Horrifed)*

Drugs?!

> BEATNIK "CAT"
> *(Growling, lighting up a joint and passing it to*
> *BEAT GIRL)*

YEAAAAAHHHHH!!

> BEAT GIRL
> *(Taking a big toke)*

LOCO-WEED!! When I'm high, man, I AM ODETTA!! LET'S GET NAKED AND SMOKE!!

BEATNIK "CAT" *passes out cold. KIDS are terrified. PENNY breaks out in loud sobs.*

> TRACY
> *(All bravado gone)*
> I WANT MY MAMA!!!

> LINK
> *(Trying to protect the girls)*
> Don't breathe it in!!! You'll be addicted!

> SEAWEED
> *(Shoving everybody out the door; to BEAT GIRL)*
> Later, sister, later! Much later!

96) *Exterior Beatnik house. Cruising by in their car are the TURN-BLADS, who stomp on brakes as soon as they see KIDS exiting. From other direction come the PINGLETONS who screech to a stop and leap out, accompanied by a stern psychiatrist, DR. FREDRIKSON. The KIDS hesitate and turn back to BEAT GIRL who begins ranting the opening lines of Allen Ginsberg's* Howl. *Wearily, the KIDS give up.*

> PENNY
> Hi, Dad.

> MR. PINGLETON
> Don't "Hi, Dad" me. The whole world saw you on the news!

> MRS. PINGLETON
> *(Sternly)*
> Penny, this is Doctor Fredrikson. He's a psychiatrist, and he is gonna make you better.

> DR. FREDRIKSON
> *(Ridiculously earnest, spinning "hypnotic wheel" at PENNY)*
> Feeling depressed, Penny? Want to talk about it? Think of all the white boys in school and how much you'd like to date one.
> *(Grabbing strait-jacket from car and holding it up)*
> Want to slip this on and be a good girl?

MRS. PINGLETON
I'm telling you, SHOCK TREATMENTS are the answer!!

PENNY *wearily slips on strait-jacket and is dragged away.*

PENNY
(Yelling back)
I LOVE YOU, SEAWEED!!

WILBUR *and* EDNA *open door of car for* TRACY.

WILBUR
Come on, honey, time to go home. You can see Link tomorrow.

EDNA
We've been worried sick about you. This neighborhood is no place
for a star! Hurry up before anyone *sees* you!

TRACY
(Meekly getting in car)
HAIR-HOPPERS FOR INTEGRATION!!!

97) *Interior Turnblad car.* WILBUR, EDNA, *and a sullen* TRACY, *are
driving home.*

EDNA
Isn't *fame* enough for a sixteen-year-old?

TRACY
No, it's not, mother!

WILBUR
This is East Baltimore, honey, not Greenwich Village.

TRACY
You're just like all the rest—a bunch of racists! There's more to life
than auto shows, teased hair, and angel blouses! I'm a Freedom
Fighter now, and I'm running away to Mississippi!!

Tammy and Corny Collins (Mink Stole, Shawn Thompson).

TRACY leaps from car as it pulls up to her house and starts to run, but is surprised by a mob of FANS, black and white, waiting outside of Hardy-Har Joke Shop, that has been turned into campaign headquarters for Tracy's candidacy for Miss Auto Show by her parents. Huge blow-ups of Tracy are in window, homemade banners reading "Tracy Needs Your Vote!" hang. FANS surround her, thrusting autograph books in her face, flashing cameras, and chanting "Vote for Tracy." TRACY tries to flee, but FANS hoist her up, cheering. Close-up of Tracy's confused face as she turns to her parents' beaming faces. Fade out.

98) Interior Tilted Acres Amusement Park. Next Day. Montage of various COUNCIL MEMBERS on rides. TRACY and LINK, holding arms in the air, scream and go down hill of roller coaster. Tracy's giant hairdo doesn't budge. LOU ANN and IQ on "Salt and Pepper Shaker." CARMELITA and CONSUELLA bumping into each other in "Dodge 'Em Cars." FENDER, SHELLY, and SHANNON on "Round-Up." AMBER rides alone on kiddie ride, feels nauseated, and then weakly vomits over the side of car.

99) Interior of the Corny Collins TV studio set up inside Tilted Acres. The show is about to go on the air live. Cameras being set up, TAMMY and CORNY doing last-minute preparations. Amusement park PATRONS stand around roped-off dance floor and gawk.

Seaweed, Motormouth, L'il Inez, and Nadine fight for justice (Clayton Prince, Ruth Brown, Cyrkle Milbourne, Dawn Hill).

100) Exterior Tilted Acres. Twenty INTEGRATION PICKETS outside park in peaceful protest. We see MOTORMOUTH, SEAWEED, NADINE, and L'IL INEZ among the racially mixed crowd. Many MINISTERS are in the demonstration. Hired THUGS block their exit. COUNTER-DEMONSTRATORS are to one side being held back by POLICE. Some are carrying Confederate flags. The PRESS is filming the entire event. The mood is extremely tense.

101) Interior Tilted Acres. FRANKLIN VON TUSSLE is being filmed by a NEWS TEAM. VELMA stands proudly beside him.

FRANKLIN
(To camera)
Personally, I have nothing against them. It's solely a matter of economy. Tilted Acres will never be integrated.

VELMA and FRANKLIN
Segregation today! Segregation tomorrow! Segregation forever!

102) Interior Corny Collins set. CORNY COLLINS and TAMMY argue with WZZT OFFICIALS. We see KIDS taking their places on dance floor in the background.

79

MR. HODGEPILE
One black face gets on camera and the show is off the air!

CORNY
The kids don't care if blacks dance on the show. Can't you see this is ripping the city apart?

TAMMY
(Pleading)
Motormouth Maybelle is out there and she's our friend. We've done hops together for years. The kids love her!

OFFICIAL B
"The Corny Collins Show" will remain white or you're all fired. Is that clear?

CORNY COLLINS rushes on camera.

CORNY
Good Afternoon, Baltimore! And welcome to "The Corny Collins Show"! We're *live* at Tilted Acres, so hop in the car, bring the whole family and come on out! Right now, I'd like to bring on camera the two top contenders in our Miss Auto Show contest. Amber Von Tussle and Tracy Turnblad!

AMBER comes on camera from the left and TRACY from the right. They both try to smile for the camera, but can't help giving each other dirty looks.

CORNY
(Continuing)
I understand you're both going to introduce a brand-new dance on the show today . . .

AMBER
(Butting in)
Yes, I am, Corny. It's called "The Limbo Rock," and I bet . . .
(Sneering at TRACY)
. . . *some* people will find it quite difficult.

103) Interior Penny Pingleton's bedroom. The bedroom door has been replaced by bars and is locked with a giant padlock. PENNY is ironing her hair on an ironing board and watching her TV as AMBER successfully goes under the limbo pole. The ridiculous psychiatrist, DR. FREDRIKSON, enters.

> DR. FREDRIKSON
>
> Good afternoon, Penny. Feeling better? Getting in touch with your anger?

> PENNY
> *(Watching TRACY go under Limbo pole with difficulty and ignoring DR. FREDRIKSON)*
>
> Lower, Tracy! Lower!

> DR. FREDRIKSON
> *(Concerned)*
>
> Do you believe all television shows are the real world? Tell me about it. What do you fantasize about this show?

> PENNY
> *(Still ironing her hair)*
>
> Oh, eat one!

104) Exterior Tilted Acres. A COUNTER-DEMONSTRATOR is shoving hot dogs in his mouth while jeering and taunting the PEACEFUL DEMONSTRATORS with racial taunts. POLICE and paddy wagons are arriving.

105) Interior Turnblad's rec room. EDNA is nauseated as she watches Amber's cutesy Limbo turn on TV while ironing. WILBUR is reading Life *magazine with a cover story on the integration movement.*

> EDNA
>
> I watch that tramp, and I'm embarrassed to be white!

> WILBUR
>
> You know, I been reading about these kids. Maybe Tracy could be some sort of campus leader . . .

> EDNA
>
> Wilbur, it's the times . . . they're a-changin'. Something is blowin' in the wind. Fetch me my diet pills, would you, hon?

"It's the times . . . they're a-changin'" (Divine, Jerry Stiller).

106) Interior Corny Collins set. We see TRACY fall going under the limbo pole. AMBER laughs and then goes under the pole obnoxiously, becoming the winner. TRACY gets up, puts on "Integration Now" button and goes back on camera with AMBER and CORNY.

> CORNY
>
> Baltimore, you saw it here first. The Limbo Rock! Thank you, Amber.

> AMBER
>
> I'm a winner, Corny!

> CORNY
>
> Well, Amber you won the dance, but let's check our election results and see how you're doing!

LOU ANN wheels out Miss Auto Show vote board.

> CORNY
> *(Continuing)*
> Ladies and gentlemen, we have an upset!

AMBER looks horrified.

CORNY
(Continuing)
For the first time, Tracy Turnblad is number one with a bullet!
What do you have to say for yourself, Tracy?

TRACY
(Beaming)
If elected, I plan to represent *all* of Baltimore.
(Some applause, some boos)
And today I'd like to introduce a dance and dedicate it to some special friends . . .

AMBER sees a large ROACH crawl from back of Tracy's lacquered hairdo and gawks in transfixed horror as TRACY, absent-mindedly, slaps it off her neck and continues talking.

TRACY
(Continuing)
. . . who, because of small-minded people, can't be here with me today. My dance is "The Waddle," it's by the Bracelets, and it goes out especially to Seaweed and Penny, a couple whose love will never be snuffed out by racism!

AMBER
(Blurting out in disgust)
This girl has roaches in her hair! I'm not kidding! I just saw one!

CORNY
(Nervously)
Oh, Amber, you ARE a comedienne.
(To camera)
Ladies and gentlemen, boys and girls, let's have a big hand for Tracy and "The Waddle."

TRACY goes to dance floor and starts expertly doing the comical dance with defiant pride.

107) Interior Turnblad's rec room. EDNA and WILBUR are furious. TRACY is "waddling" on TV screen.

> EDNA
ROACHES!?? My little Tracy is a clean teen!

> WILBUR
There's no bugs on our baby!

> EDNA
> *(Haughtily)*
She washes her hair weekly. Why she's practically a "Breck girl"!

108) Exterior Tilted Acres. PICKETS are advancing on entrance.

> TILTED ACRES THUG
> *(Through bullhorn)*
This is private property! You are trespassing!

Racist COUNTER-DEMONSTRATOR lights cherry bomb and throws it into CROWD. Panic. POLICE start moving in. SEAWEED, MOTOR-MOUTH, L'IL INEZ, and NADINE caught in middle of budding race riot. Some MINISTERS go limp, RACISTS break through police lines and chase DEMONSTRATORS who overcome SECURITY GUARDS and rush into amusement park.

109) Interior Tilted Acres. WHITE FAMILIES scream in panic at the sight of BLACKS hopping on Tilt-A-Whirl. L'IL INEZ hops on kiddie ride and WHITE FAMILIES snatch their KIDS away. POLICE run into the park, swinging billy clubs.

110) Interior Corny Collins set. LINK and TRACY do "Waddle" on dance floor as race riot goes on in the background. KIDS on show start to panic and run. CORNY and TAMMY are trying to preserve calm. WZZT OFFICIALS are trying to get show off the air. CAMERAMEN are filming anyway. SEAWEED and NADINE are held back from entering dance area by RACISTS and COPS. TRACY is cheering them on, dancing in a frenzy. AMBER panics and runs.

111) Interior Tilted Acres. AMBER is running in terror through full-fledged race riot, and spots her horrified PARENTS and runs to them. Trapped, they run to Dodge 'Em Cars to hide out; FRANKLIN and VELMA in one car, AMBER in the other. They circle the ring ridiculously. MOTORMOUTH MAYBELLE spots them, hops in another Dodge 'Em Car and gives chase. FRANKLIN and VELMA desperately floor the accelerator looking over their shoulders. MOTORMOUTH finally corners AMBER who is desperately trying to control her careening-in-reverse Dodge 'Em Car. MOTORMOUTH aims her car slowly, floors it, and bangs into Amber's car so hard it flies back into Von Tussle's car and knocks them silly. MOTORMOUTH roars in laughter. COPS enter, try to drag MOTORMOUTH away, struggle to lift her, and finally give up.

112) Interior Corny Collins set. TRACY and LINK are still dancing. COUNTER-DEMONSTRATORS invade the set, blocking BLACKS who try to get through to dance. CORNY is decked by HILLBILLY right on the air.

113) Interior Turnblad's rec room. They stare at TV screen in horror.

WILBUR

Run, baby!! Run!

EDNA

Maybe she'll get in *Life* magazine.

114) Interior Penny's bedroom.

PENNY
(Watching excitedly, falling to knees to pray)

Oh, please, God! I'll never tease my hair again! PLEASE let "The Corny Collins Show" be integrated!

DR. FREDRIKSON shakes his head, gets doctor bag.

115) Interior Corny Collins set. SEAWEED is clubbed by COP and knocked to the ground. TAMMY is menaced by approaching SLOB REDNECK WOMAN who is swinging her pocketbook as a lethal weapon. She conks TAMMY on the head and knocks her out. Each time pocketbook hits someone, ridiculous, exaggerated sound effects are heard. SLOB REDNECK WOMAN twirls her pocketbook "weapon" yelling karate sounds and daring anybody to take her on. LINK hesitates and then charges her, but SLOB REDNECK WOMAN expertly "kneecaps" him on each leg with pocketbook and he falls to ground. SLOB REDNECK WOMAN turns to TRACY and approaches with pocketbook terrifyingly twirling. SLOB REDNECK WOMAN swings pocketbook but TRACY expertly blocks the bag, spits in SLOB REDNECK WOMAN'S eye, knees her in the crotch, grabs pocketbook straps, *wraps them around SLOB RED-NECK WOMAN'S neck, and begins strangling her.*

116) *Interior Turnblad's rec room.*

WILBUR
(Watching, terrified)
They'll give her the electric chair now!

EDNA
Suppose they burn down our house . . . ?

117) *Interior Penny's bedroom. Riot is on TV screen. COPS are invading the set.*

PENNY
Police brutality! Police brutality!

DR. FREDRIKSON *sneaks up to* PENNY *with electric cattle prod and touches it to her skin to shock her. Sparks fly out.*

DR. FREDRIKSON

Negroes.

(Shocking her again)

Black boys.

PENNY
OUCH!! You pervert! You quack!

DR. FREDRIKSON
(Chasing her)
That's what happens when we act bad! Electricity will teach you!
(Shocking her)

Colored people.

PENNY
SEAWEED! I'M HOT FOR YOU!!

118) *Interior Corny Collins set. A complete race riot. TRACY is pulled off SLOB REDNECK WOMAN by two MEAN COPS, who handcuff her and throw her into paddy wagon. LINK is crawling with injured legs toward paddy wagon.*

LINK

TRACY!! TRACY!!

Door of paddy wagon slams shut. Fade out.

119) Fade in to Exterior Penny's parents' house. Night. SEAWEED, in head bandage, sneaks up and PENNY drops a rope of knotted sheets through bars. SEAWEED climbs up, carrying a pair of large wire cutters. PENNY kisses him through bars and nervously watches him cut through and enter bedroom.

120) Interior Penny's bedroom. SEAWEED and PENNY embrace. The eleven o'clock news comes on.

ANNOUNCER

Good evening. Wednesday, June 2nd, 1962. Racially tense Tilted Acres Amusement Park, long a tradition of Baltimore fun, opened its doors today and closed them four hours later.

PENNY and SEAWEED rush to TV set to watch.

ANNOUNCER
(Continuing)

What started out as a peaceful demonstration against the owner's segregated admission policy soon escalated into a full-fledged race riot during an on-location shooting of the popular TV dance party, "The Corny Collins Show." One of the dancers on the program and a possible queen of the upcoming Auto Show . . .

We see TRACY being thrown in paddy wagon.

ANNOUNCER
(Continuing)

. . . was arrested and held at Montrose Reformatory for Girls.

121) Interior Montrose Reformatory for Girls. TRACY, in prison uniform, is surrounded by BLACK TEEN INMATES watching news on pitifully old TV set. She is having her hair ironed by another INMATE. They see shot of TRACY on TV.

INMATE

Girl, they gonna flip when they see THE NEW YOU!

ANNOUNCER

... Link Larkin, another popular dancer on the show and common-law boyfriend of Miss Turnblad ...

TRACY kneels in front of TV.

ANNOUNCER
(Continuing)

... was listed in fair condition at Union Memorial Hospital tonight ...

Shot of LINK in hospital bed.

ANNOUNCER
(Continuing)

... recovering from two broken knee-caps received in one of the many incidents of violence that erupted today.

LINK
(On screen)

I love you, Tracy.

TRACY
(Sobbing, kissing TV screen)

I love you too, Link. We'll be together soon ... in an integrated society.
(To INMATES)
God, I hope he likes my hair!

Screen changes to close-up of AMBER. TRACY jumps back.

122) Interior Von Tussle's living room. FRANKLIN and VELMA are hard at work making a small bomb out of explosives and an alarm clock, as they both watch TV news.

AMBER
(On TV)

Tracy Turnblad is a human roach nest! Is this the caliber of teenager we want representing Baltimore at the Auto Show?

VELMA

Amber will be so proud of us.

FRANKLIN

We're going to go down in the history books for this one, Velma.

123) Interior Turnblad rec room. MOTORMOUTH MAYBELLE and L'IL INEZ have joined an awkward WILBUR and EDNA as they nervously watch the TV news. L'IL INEZ hops on Wilbur's lap, wearing a Hardy-Har arrow through her head. We see CORNY COLLINS being interviewed. He is beaten up.

ANNOUNCER

. . . Corny Collins, host of the controversial show, has gone on the record in favor of integrating his dancers.

CORNY

Integration is what's happening today. I'm *proud* of Tracy Turnblad!

ANNOUNCER

. . . Tracy's parents, Edna and Wilbur Turnblad, had an emotional appeal for their daughter . . .

124) Interior Penny's bedroom. PENNY and SEAWEED watch, PENNY checking nervously for her mother's approach.

EDNA
(On TV)
Tracy, honey, we know you are innocent. You were right all along about integration. We've joined the NAACP . . .

WILBUR
(On TV)
. . . and we will *fight* in every way possible to get you released and back in front of the cameras where you belong.
(Squirts NEWS INTERVIEWER with water from a trick bow-tie)
Integration is no laughing matter!

We hear MRS. PINGLETON call out for PENNY from downstairs.
PENNY panics, and SEAWEED hides under the bed. PENNY composes
herself and continues watching the news. We see MOTORMOUTH on
TV in front of her record shop.

ANNOUNCER

Motormouth Maybelle, a local DJ and participant in today's riot,
had this to say . . .

MOTORMOUTH

It's time for black and white to join hands and show our Governor
that we will not stand for racism. Several demonstrations are planned
tomorrow to protest the unfair arrest of this brave teenager.
(To camera)
Free Tracy Turnblad! Free Tracy Turnblad!

Dr. Fredrikson (John Waters)

TV camera pulls back to show MOTORMOUTH surrounded by black and white chanting DEMONSTRATORS.

MRS. PINGLETON unlocks Penny's "cell" door and enters bedroom, flicking off the TV.

MRS. PINGLETON
(Trying a new tactic, being nice)
Aren't you glad you're punished and under psychiatric care? You could have been killed today.

PENNY
(Eyeing opened and unlocked bedroom door)
I wish I was at a hootenanny in Harlem!

SEAWEED laughs out loud under the bed.

MRS. PINGLETON
What was that?

PENNY
Nothing.

MRS. PINGLETON
I heard somebody laugh.
(Getting on her knees and seeing SEAWEED)
Oh, my God! There are colored people in my house!

SEAWEED jumps from under the bed, grabs PENNY, and they escape through the still-opened door.

MRS. PINGLETON
(Continuing)
I'm making a citizen's arrest! Stop! Stop! In the name of the law!

125) Interior Pingleton living room. MR. PINGLETON is in a recliner and reading a newspaper with the headline "Riot at Tilted Acres." He hears commotion and jumps up as PENNY and SEAWEED barrel down steps with MRS. PINGLETON in hot pursuit.

MRS. PINGLETON

PADDY!! Stop them!

MR. PINGLETON

What the? . . . Hey!

MR. PINGLETON *tries to grab them, but after a brief skirmish, PENNY and SEAWEED escape out the front door.*

126) *Exterior Pingleton's row house. SEAWEED and PENNY are chased by MR. PINGLETON who finally gives up.*

MR. PINGLETON

Penny Pingleton! I'm calling the cops! You are no longer my daughter! YOU ARE PUNISHED, EVEN AFTER YOU DIE!

MRS. PINGLETON
(Sobbing on front porch)

Who would have ever thought . . . My daughter a beatnik, practically ready for the Rat Pack . . . She's . . . she's . . . the May Britt of Baltimore.
(Yelling off in the distance)
WHO'S NEXT IN MY HOUSE? SAMMY DAVIS JR?!!

127) *Interior Nadine's club basement. NADINE is listening to "Hot Nuts" by Dave Clark and the Hot Nuts and reading* Jet *magazine. We hear a tap on basement door, and NADINE suspiciously answers it. We see SEAWEED and PENNY, but NADINE blocks their way.*

NADINE

No way, Seaweed! I never had no white girls in my basement, and I don't plan on it now!

SEAWEED
(Pleading)

Let us in, Nadine. We have nowhere to go! The first place they'll look is my mom's.

PENNY

You owe it to the Movement, Nadine.

They push their way in.

NADINE

My mom will kill me. We may not be wealthy, but we have a clean house. Everybody knows hair-hoppers have roaches in their hair!

PENNY

I don't *use* hairspray anymore. Can't you see? I've gone "Joe College."

NADINE

Once a hair-hopper, always a hair-hopper in my book! If you're gonna stay in my club basement, I'm gonna have to spray.
(Getting an oversized roach-repellent spray gun)
Come on, or back out in the street where you belong.

SEAWEED

You're being counter-revolutionary.

PENNY

And I'm telling Coretta King when I finally get to meet her.

NADINE

Don't be so smart mouthed, Miss Rock 'n' Roach!
(Spraying)
A roach is a roach. And they multiply and multiply and, first thing you know, they'll be eating my records!

We hear door open from upstairs.

MOTHER

Nadine, who you talking to down there?

NADINE

(Scared)
Nobody, Ma. It's just the record.

MOTHER, an imposing black woman, comes down basement steps as PENNY and SEAWEED hide.

MOTHER
I hope I didn't hear no dirty records playing down here!

NADINE
It's just the "Hot Nuts," Ma. It's a comedy album.

MOTHER
Watch your mouth, Nadine!

MOTHER *approaches record player; puts needle down and hears obscene lyric from album.*

MOTHER
(Continuing)
You think that's comedy, Nadine?

MOTHER *snatches off record and breaks it in two.*

MOTHER
(Continuing)
No wonder there's so much trouble today what with this filth for teenagers. Can't you listen to Mahalia Jackson or somebody with some talent?
(Seeing Penny's ankle boot sticking out from hiding place)
Oooooooh! Sweet Jesus! There's a white person in my house!

MOTHER *picks up roach spray and starts spraying SEAWEED and PENNY in their faces. PENNY and SEAWEED grope for the door, blinded.*

MOTHER
(To PENNY)
GET OUT YOU VERMIN! YOU YELLOW DEVIL!

SEAWEED and PENNY *stagger out back door, temporarily blinded, chased by Nadine's MOTHER. NADINE is sobbing, trying to put the record back together. Fade out.*

128) Fade in to Exterior Auto Show. CROWDS *filing in.*

129) *Interior Auto Show. The GOVERNOR is cutting the ribbon for opening as PRESS films. CROWDS applaud and admire next year's cars on display. HAIR-HOPPER MODELS pose for cheesecake on new cars as SALESMEN give out literature. LITTLE KIDS marvel at "futuristic" models.*

Cut to Miss Auto Show 1962 throne. Camera pulls back to reveal makeshift set for on-location "Corny Collins Show." A WZZT OFFICIAL is sternly tabulating last-minute ballots for the contest. We see AMBER excitedly spraying her hair and touching up her makeup. TAMMY is hurriedly getting kids to their places for the beginning of the show. CORNY is shaking hands and posing for the press with GOVERNOR.

130) *Interior Montrose Reform School. TRACY with her ironed flat hairdo is tuning into the show surrounded by BLACK TEEN INMATES. A GUARD watches them sternly. TRACY is miserable, and fellow INMATES comfort her. "The Corny Collins Show" comes on TV.*

CORNY
. . . well, Baltimore, today's the big day. We're live at the Fifth Regiment Armory for the grand opening of the 1962 Auto Show. And who will be the dancin' princess from our Council to be crowned queen?

131) *Interior Auto Show. GOVERNOR leaves, shaking hands, being filmed, and we see his face turn to horror as he nears exit and is confronted by about TEN ANGRY PICKETS, held back by SECURITY GUARD. We see EDNA, WILBUR, and BLACK and WHITE KIDS chanting, "Free Tracy Turnblad! Free Tracy Turnblad!" and carrying picket signs reading, "Free Our Queen," "Hair-Hoppers for Integration" and "Auto Show Racism." WILBUR gives out noisemakers, kazoos, etc. from his large "Hardy-Har" shopping bag. GOVERNOR looks appalled and pushes his way through them with an AIDE and exits.*

132) *Interior Governor's limousine.*

GOVERNOR
Who the *hell* is Tracy Turnblad?

                         AIDE
                  (Reading from notes)
She is an upper-lower class teenager who became a dancing star on
"The Corny Collins Show." She was arrested in yesterday's demon-
stration at Tilted Acres and is currently being held at Montrose
Reformatory for Girls. She is a hair-hopper.

                       GOVERNOR
. . . a *what*?

133) *Exterior Governor's mansion. We see many PICKETS out front,
including MOTORMOUTH MAYBELLE and L'IL INEZ, marching,
singing "We Shall Overcome" as TV CREW film them.*

134) *Interior Governor's limousine, pulling up in front of his mansion.*

                       GOVERNOR
Jesus Christ! Teenage pickets! A political hot potato, and I wasn't
even warned!

                         AIDE
This came out of nowhere. We had no idea of her grassroots
support.

                       GOVERNOR
Keep the goddamn cops away before this makes the national news!!

135) *Exterior Governor's mansion. As GOVERNOR opens door to
step out, DEMONSTRATORS run to lie down and block his path.
They sing "We Shall Overcome" as GOVERNOR gingerly tries to step
over them, smiling for the news cameras, mumbling, "Excuse me," "I
beg your pardon." COPS are on hand but he motions for them to step
back. Suddenly MOTORMOUTH MAYBELLE and L'IL INEZ reach
up as he tries to step over them and handcuff themselves to each of
Governor's wrists. ALL DEMONSTRATORS leap up and form two-
sided line to Governor's door, shouting, "Free Tracy Turnblad."
CAMERA CREWS go wild and GOVERNOR tries to retain a sem-
blance of dignity as he walks to his mansion, chained to his new
chanting "appendages."*

136) *Interior Governor's mansion. Prim and proper FIRST LADY rushes down steps in a panic to greet him. GOVERNOR enters, chained to MOTORMOUTH and L'IL INEZ. FIRST LADY stops in her tracks.*

GOVERNOR
(Stupidly)

Honey, I'm home.

MOTORMOUTH and L'IL INEZ

Free Tracy Turnblad! Free Tracy Turnblad!

137) *Exterior Von Tussle house. About TEN PICKETS are marching in front of house, chanting, "Free Tracy Turnblad," and carrying placards that read "Tilted Acres is Racist," "Amber is an Asshole," "Von Tussles are Fascists." We see PENNY and SEAWEED among the crowd disguised as nuns.*

138) *Interior Von Tussle house. VELMA is seated in front of a makeup mirror as FRANKLIN very carefully places home-made bomb inside her giant, new hairdo.*

FRANKLIN
(Arranging huge curl over alarm clock)

Now, remember, if AMBER loses, she walks off the set and you throw the bomb. BOOM!!

VELMA
(Holding her head very still)

JUST BE CAREFUL!!

139) *Exterior Von Tussle House. VELMA and FRANKLIN exit wearing gas masks. PICKETS jeer. FRANKLIN throws tear gas bomb at DEMONSTRATORS who flee, coughing and rubbing their eyes. Velma's giant, three-foot hairdo hides the bomb and she walks to car steadily and struggles to fit hairdo in car.*

140) *Interior Auto Show. We see CORNY on camera with LINK in wheelchair.*

Planting the bomb (Sonny Bono, Debbie Harry).

CORNY

Link, I know you're in great pain, but I understand there's something you'd like to do on the show today.

LINK

Yes, Corny . . . I'd like to try and dance!

All COUNCIL MEMBERS tearfully applaud, except AMBER.

LINK
(Continuing)
I'd love to dedicate it to the girl I love . . .

141) Interior Montrose Reform School. TRACY is kneeling in front of TV, tears of happiness cascading down her cheeks.

LINK
(To camera)
. . . Tracy Turnblad, if you're out there watching, you'll always be Miss Auto Show in my mind. This one's for you!

TRACY

You can do it, my darling!

TRACY French-kisses the TV.

CORNY
(On TV)
Ladies and gentlemen, a "Corny Collins" first! The Van Dykes' brand new record, "Stupidity."

142) Interior Auto Show. LINK is struggling to get out of wheelchair.

CORNY

Can you make it, Link?

LINK
(Hobbling to dance floor)
I'll . . . try . . . Corny.

CORNY

A BIG HAND FOR LINK LARKIN!!

We hear Van Dykes' "Stupidity" play and LINK starts doing his comedy gimmick dance, featuring idiot expressions and spastic dance steps. At first he is in great pain, but as dance continues, he builds in physical power.

143) Interior Montrose Reform School. TRACY is doing "Stupidity" dance with BLACK TEEN INMATES. Even MEAN MATRON has joined in. Suddenly, a NEWS ANNOUNCER flashes on screen.

ANNOUNCER

We have a bulletin! Governor Tawes has been taken hostage by a 250-pound woman identified as local DJ Motormouth Maybelle, and her ten-year-old daughter Inez. As of this report, both demonstrators are still handcuffed to the Governor's wrists inside his mansion demanding the release of sixteen-year-old Tracy Turnblad from Montrose Reformatory for Girls. Now, back to our regular programming.

TRACY and BLACK TEEN INAMTES cheer in shocked happiness.

144) Interior Governor's bedroom. He is sitting on bed with MOTOR-MOUTH and L'IL INEZ, who watch "Corny Collins Show" on TV. We hear dance end and see on-screen LINK as he collapses back in wheel-chair. FIRST LADY holds phone to governor's ear and smiles politely at DEMONSTRATORS sprawled on her bed.

GOVERNOR

Absolutely not! No cops! No cameras! We're going to work this out . . .
(To MOTORMOUTH)
. . . aren't we . . . madam? You *do* have the key, don't you?

MOTORMOUTH

We'll talk about the key when you release Tracy!
(To FIRST LADY)
You got anything to eat?

FIRST LADY
(Startled, trying to be polite)
Would milk and cookies be all right?

L'IL INEZ
YEEEAAAAH! I'm hungry. And hurry up, would you?

145) Interior Auto Show. EDNA and WILBUR are chanting, shaking noisemakers, and picketing with other DEMONSTRATORS. VELMA and FRANKLIN enter, shoving their way through picket line to boos and jeers from INTEGRATIONISTS, protected by SECURITY GUARDS.

We see FRANKLIN and VELMA approach set and smile evilly at AMBER who waves back nervously.

CORNY
And now for the moment of truth!

BAND begins drumroll.

CORNY
(Continuing)
You, the audience, have made your decision . . .

We see shot of SEAWEED and PENNY, still disguised as nuns, entering Auto Show. They wink at EDNA and WILBUR and tail VON TUSSLES. FAMILIES greet them reverently with "Good afternoon, sisters," and drop money into their offering baskets. PENNY and SEAWEED make their way to TV show set and stand next to VELMA and FRANKLIN who smile at them and make Sign of Cross.

CORNY
(Continuing)
. . . and to announce the results, we have with us Mr. Arvin Hodgepile, President of WZZT Studios . . .

MR. HODGEPILE enters in a stiff suit and tie to polite applause.

MR. HODGEPILE
Thank you. We have a difficult situation with the vote tabulation . . .

CROWD starts buzzing quizzically. AMBER sweats. VELMA looks worried and takes a hairpin out of her hairdo. PENNY and SEAWEED watch FRANKLIN and VELMA, sensing trouble.

MR. HODGEPILE
(Continuing)
... the results were quite close ...

146) *Interior Montrose Reform School. Close-up of TRACY nervously watching as BLACK TEEN INMATES chant, "Tracy! Tracy! Tracy!"*

147) *Interior Auto Show. PICKETS are shouting "Tracy! Tracy! Tracy! Tracy!" WILBUR and EDNA are the loudest and most carried away.*

MR. HODGEPILE
(Reading from notes)
Unfortunately ... the technical winner ... is ... Tracy Turnblad ... but ...

He is interrupted by wild applause and cheering. COUNCIL goes nuts. AMBER is stunned. LINK hops from wheelchair. Even CORNY and TAMMY start cheering. MR. PINKY jumps up and down holding sign, "She's a Hefty Hideaway Girl!" PICKETS go berserk cheering. EDNA and WILBUR are ecstatic and hug.

148) *Interior Montrose Reform School. Wild celebration. TRACY is hoisted with some difficulty to a cheering BLACK TEEN INMATE'S shoulders.*

149) *Interior Governor's bedroom. L'IL INEZ is jumping up and down in childhood delirium. MOTORMOUTH grabs GOVERNOR and, before horrified FIRST LADY, gives him a big kiss.*

150) *Interior Auto show. Pandemonium. AMBER is in a sore loser temper tantrum, kicking other COUNCIL MEMBERS, weeping. A furious VELMA and FRANKLIN are next to cheering nuns, SEAWEED and PENNY. FRANKLIN nods to VELMA and she begins frantically taking out hairpins to get to bomb. FRANKLIN tries to get Amber's attention. PENNY stops cheering and intently watches VELMA. She nudges SEA-WEED who also watches and notices a tiny section of the bomb barely visible as VELMA removes the first of many hairpieces. SEAWEED and PENNY try to exit, fighting their way through crowd to integration PICKETS and whisper to WILBUR. WILBUR tries to rush to VON TUS-SLES but is blocked by GUARD. MR. HODGEPILE tries to quiet the cheering CROWD.*

> MR. HODGEPILE
> *(Frantically)*
> Wait a minute! Quiet! Quiet! Shut up or we're going off the air!

CROWD *finally quiets down.*

> MR. HODGEPILE
> *(Continuing)*
> Now listen carefully. Since Miss Turnblad is in reform school, the judges have ruled her ineligible. WZZT is proud to announce the winner of Miss Auto Show 1962—AMBER VON TUSSLE!

AMBER'S *face turns to joy as she runs stage center, sobbing to horrendous boos from the CROWD. LINK collapses and crawls painfully back to wheelchair. VELMA and FRANKLIN smile in happy surprise. VELMA starts replacing hairpins and layers of hairpieces over bomb. WILBUR and EDNA are furious, begin loudly demonstrating once again. AMBER is being helped into futuristic mini-car promotional prop and she drives around set waving happily to jeering CROWD as BAND plays victory number. LINK is sobbing in wheelchair. Even the COUNCIL boos her.*

151) *Interior Montrose Reform School.* TRACY *and* BLACK TEEN INMATES *are attacking TV showing Amber's futuristic car ride, kicking the screen, trying to destroy it.* MATRON *is pulling them off.*

152) *Interior Governor's bedroom.* MOTORMOUTH *and* L'IL INEZ *are torturing the* GOVERNOR *by smothering him with kisses.* FIRST LADY *is vainly trying to tempt them off with cookies. Finally,* GOVERNOR *can stand it no more.*

> GOVERNOR
> Okay! UNCLE! UNCLE! You win! Give me the goddamn phone! For Christ's sake, pardon Tracy Turnblad!

153) *Interior Auto Show.* AMBER *is being helped out of her "car" by* MR. HODGEPILE *and is led over to* CORNY *on the air.* MR. HODGEPILE *places the Miss Auto Show crown on her head.* CROWD *boos.*

CORNY

Well, Amber, like it or not, you are officially Miss Auto Show 1962.
Congratulations. Any words for your opponent who many feel was
the popular winner?

AMBER

I'd like to lead a dance and dedicate it to that loser!
(To camera)
Tracy Turnblad, I hope you're watching because this one's for you.
It's a brand-new dance, one that I'm *sure* you'll know how to do!
It's called "The Roach"! Too bad you can't be here to do it!

*AMBER goes to stage center and we hear "The Roach" by Gene and
Wendell. AMBER theatrically does the dance which consists of squashing
motions with the feet and spraying motions with the hands.*

*154) Interior Montrose Reform School. Close-up of battered TV screen.
AMBER is "squishing" to the chorus of the song, "Kill that roach,"
jeering at Tracy on camera. TRACY is being held by MATRONS in a near
psychotic rage. Suddenly the TV screen cuts to NEWS ANNOUNCER.*

ANNOUNCER

We have another bulletin. Governor Tawes has ordered the release
of Tracy Turnblad. I repeat. Governor Tawes has ordered . . .

BLACK TEEN INMATES go wild. Tracy's fit turns to happy disbelief.

*155) Exterior Reform School. "The Roach" is still playing on soundtrack.
MOB of black and white fans await Tracy's release. Suddenly, doors swing
open and TRACY exits wildly doing "The Roach." Cop car pulls up and
MOTORMOUTH and L'IL INEZ hop out, dancing to insane applause.
Even COP starts dancing. MOB goes crazy. TRACY, still dancing, leads
the happy MOB toward Auto Show, everyone dancing in glee.*

*156) Interior Auto Show. "The Roach" is ending. Suddenly, TRACY and
MOB, MOTORMOUTH, and L'IL INEZ burst through doors, knocking
down SECURITY GUARD and flood into studio to wild applause.
EDNA and WILBUR hug their daughter and DEMONSTRATORS
invade Auto Show. WILBUR runs to VON TUSSLES, throws fake snakes
at VELMA and shoots FRANKLIN with a water pistol. FRANKLIN and
VELMA try to flee him but WILBUR follows.*

AMBER *sees TRACY, stops dancing in her tracks, runs to throne and hops in defiantly, holding on for dear life.* CORNY *and* TAMMY *are thrilled at Tracy's arrival and cheer.* LINK *springs out of wheelchair and runs to embrace her.* TAMMY *grabs* CORNY *and gives him a big kiss.* WZZT OFFICIALS *throw up their hands in defeat and run for their lives.* MR. PINKY *runs to get Auto Show gown he has designed. We see a few* GIRL COUNCIL MEMBERS *hastily combing out hairdos, trying to imitate Tracy's flat hair.* TAMMY *hastily plays "The Push 'n' Kick" by Mark Valentino and* DEMONSTRATORS, *both black and white, rush on camera and start doing the gimmick dance.* EDNA *joins in.* PENNY *and* SEAWEED *rip off their nuns' outfits and are the first integrated couple on the air.*

VELMA *hurriedly signals to* AMBER *to get off the set, but* WILBUR *is right on top of* VELMA.

MOTORMOUTH *and* CORNY *rush to each other, kiss and embrace and* CORNY *victoriously comes on camera.*

> CORNY
> Baltimore, you've seen HISTORY being made today! Black and white together for the first time on local TV! All thanks to the real winner of today's contest—TRACY TURNBLAD!! "The Corny Collins Show" is now integrated!!

Thunderous applause. LINK *and* TRACY *kiss on camera.* FRANKLIN *screams to* AMBER *for her to escape as* VELMA *hurriedly fumbles to undo layers of hairdos for the bomb.*

Shot of AMBER *defiantly shaking her head negatively to parents, stubbornly clutching on to throne.*

TRACY TURNBLAD, now dressed in Mr. Pinky's pink roach-print gown, takes her place next to CORNY *on camera.*

> TRACY
> *(Wiping away a beauty-queen tear)*
> Thank you. Thank you. I LOVE YOU, BALTIMORE!

Deafening applause.

TRACY
(Continuing)
I don't know about you, but I FEEL LIKE DANCING! It's a brand-new dance I learned in reform school. If you've ever been down, ever been *itching* to get out, you can do it too! I've got ants in my pants, roaches in my hair, and bugs in my brain.
(Looking at AMBER)
This one's dedicated to you, baby! I'VE GOT THE BUG!

All the COUNCIL, many DEMONSTRATORS, LINK, SEAWEED and PENNY, EDNA, MR. PINKY, MOTORMOUTH, and L'IL INEZ form a giant circle and clap as TRACY jumps in the middle. "The Bug" begins playing. TRACY starts undulating, itching and scratching like a hound dog. At certain note in the song, dancer in the middle of the ring, throws "the bug" to someone else and it's their turn to hop in, picking imaginary bugs out of their hair, from underneath their clothing, or off their "crawling" skin.

Dance finale begins. Each character jumps into the ring doing "The Bug"—first LINK dancing with TRACY, then PENNY, SEAWEED, MOTORMOUTH, L'IL INEZ, EDNA, MR. PINKY, even TAMMY and CORNY and one of the CAMERAMEN. MEMBERS OF AUTO SHOW all dance "The Bug." Intercut with Amber's horrified face, FRANKLIN hurrying VELMA to get the bomb—both fleeing WILBUR. WILBUR reaches into his bag of tricks and takes out can marked "itching powder" and throws it on VELMA and FRANKLIN who start scratching uncontrollably.

Suddenly, on the note of "The Bug" in song, bomb goes off and, in slow motion, we see Velma's hairdo fly through the air. L'IL INEZ knocks the crown from Amber's head and Velma's "hairdo" lands squarely on top of Amber's head as a wig. AMBER leaps from throne and starts doing her own horrified version of "The Bug," freaking out, trying to rip off "hairdo."

We see VELMA, bald-headed, face blackened, like a Tom and Jerry cartoon, staggering around, stunned, itching and scratching as FRANKLIN is tearing off his itching-powder-covered clothes. WILBUR triumphantly jumps in dance ring and starts "bugging" with EDNA. We see VELMA

Itching powder.

"The Bug."

and FRANKLIN *being dragged away by* COPS. SOME DANCERS *break away from circle and surround Amber's freak-out "Bug," clapping and dancing.*

LINK *leads his queen* TRACY *to the throne, both "bugging," and she hops in, itching and scratching as a "bugging"* CORNY *and* TAMMY *crown her Miss Auto Show. Final shot is* TRACY *on throne, beaming, "bugging," and happily waving to entire Auto Show.*

                    TRACY
          (To ALL)
     LET'S DANCE!!

CREDITS ROLL

A DREAMLAND PRODUCTION

FEMALE TROUBLE

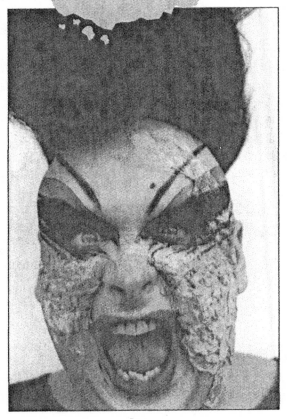

Divine

CAST

DAWN DAVENPORT . . . . DIVINE
EARL PETERSON . . . . DIVINE
DONALD DASHER . . . . DAVID LOCHARY
DONNA DASHER . . . . MARY VIVIAN PEARCE
TAFFY DAVENPORT . . . . MINK STOLE
IDA NELSON . . . . EDITH MASSEY
CONCETTA . . . . COOKIE MUELLER
CHICLET . . . . SUSAN WALSH
GATOR . . . . MICHAEL POTTER
WINK . . . . ED PERANIO
BUTTERFLY . . . . PAUL SWIFT
DRIBBLES . . . . GEORGE FIGGS
VIKKI . . . . SUSAN LOWE
TEACHER . . . . GEORGE HULSE
DAWN'S FATHER . . . . ROLAND HERTZ
DAWN'S MOTHER . . . . BETTY WOODS
TAFFY AS CHILD . . . . HILARY TAYLOR
MR. WILROY . . . . CHANNING WILROY
DEFENSE ATTORNEY . . . . SEYMOUR AVIGDOR
ERNIE . . . . BOB ADAMS
REDHEAD PRISONER . . . . PAT MORAN
CHERYL . . . . MARINA MELIN
EARNESTINE . . . . ELIZABETH COFFEY
MATRON A . . . . CHRIS MASON
MATRON B . . . . MUMME
CHAPLAN . . . . GEORGE STOVER

CREW

PRODUCTION CHIEF . . . . PAT MORAN
SETS. . . . . VINCE PERANIO
COSTUMES AND MAKEUP . . . . VAN SMITH
SOUND . . . . ROBERT MAIER
LIGHTING . . . . DAVID INSLEY
EDITING . . . . CHARLES ROGGERO

1) *Main title credits. High-contrast portraits of each of the main charac-*
ters appear with the star's name. Crew credits continue, displayed over
significant props and signature fabrics from the sets. We hear Divine on
soundtrack singing the title song, "Female Trouble."

"Female Trouble"

Chorus
I got lots of problems
Female Trouble
Maybe I'm twisted
Female Trouble.

They say I'm insane
But I don't care
Go ahead, put me
In your electric chair.

Chorus

Hey, spare me your morals
Look, everyone dies
What pleases me
Is hom-homicide!

Chorus

I'm berserk!
I like it fine
As long as I'm
Grabbing headlines.

Chorus

2) *Title card. "DAWN DAVENPORT: YOUTH 1960." Interior high*
school corridor filled with lockers. Young FEMALE STUDENTS hurry
to classes, chatting and carrying their books. DAWN DAVENPORT, a
very fat teenager, approaches her locker. She is wearing a pleated skirt,
sweater, and black, pointy-toed shoes. She has a "bubble" hairdo,
bleached orange in the front, and wears white lipstick. A "passion mark"
is obvious on her neck.

As DAWN *puts her books in her locker, another rough-looking teenager,* CONCETTA, *approaches.* CONCETTA *wears heavy makeup, a skin-tight black skirt, and a white, ruffled blouse.*

CONCETTA

Morning, Dawn.

DAWN

Hi.

CONCETTA

Hey, I like that skirt.

DAWN

Thanks.

CONCETTA

My old lady's supposed to get me one for Christmas if she's not too dumb to find it.

DAWN

Oh, Concetta, I know what you mean. My parents better get me them cha-cha heels I asked for, that's all I can say . . .
(Heightening her teased hairdo with her fingers)
Hey, hon, you got any spray net? My hair's fallin' right off my head.

CONCETTA
(Handing her a can of Aqua Net)
Sure, hon. Did you do your Geography homework?

DAWN
(Slamming her locker)
Fuck, no! Fuck homework! Who cares if we fail? I want to quit—and I am, right after I get my Christmas presents.

3) *Interior typical public school classroom.* MR. WINEBURGER, *the teacher, calls the roll and the* BORED STUDENTS *respond.*

MR. WINEBURGER

Duncan?

                    DUNCAN
Here.

                    MR. WINEBURGER
Dune?

                    DUNE
Here.

                    MR. WINEBURGER
Fryer?

*CHICLET FRYER is fixing her huge hairdo and not paying any attention.
She has pimples, wears a pink sweater, with too many buttons undone,
and looks like a tramp.*

                    MR. WINEBURGER
                    (Continuing)
Miss Fryer, are you hard of hearing?

                    CHICLET
                    (Looking up; rudely)
Here!

                    MR. WINEBURGER
                    (Approaching Chiclet)
Stand up, please . . .

CHICLET stands.

                    MR. WINEBURGER
                    (Continuing)
What on earth are you wearing? This is not Halloween.

                    CHICLET
                    (Chewing gum)
It's just a skirt and a sweater.

                    MR. WINEBURGER
Button those buttons, young lady! I bet your mother didn't see you
dressed like that.

> CHICLET
> *(Sullenly buttoning her sweater)*

It's hot in here.

> MR. WINEBURGER

That will be all. This is a classroom, not a cocktail lounge, Miss Fryer. Take this dress code violation slip home and have it signed by your parents. And, take that gum out of your mouth, for the *tenth* time. If I catch you with gum in your mouth one more time, you will be in detention for a month, do you understand?

> CHICLET
> *(Taking a huge wad of gum from her mouth and holding it in her hand)*

I understand, Mr. Wineburger!

DAWN and CONCETTA enter the classroom.

> MR. WINEBURGER

You're late, young ladies.

DAWN and CONCETTA groan and make rude faces as they take their seats and wave to their friend, CHICLET.

> MR. WINEBURGER
> *(Continuing)*

Now class, before letting you go for the holiday season, we're going to have a pop quiz.

The whole CLASS groans.

> MR. WINEBURGER
> *(Continuing)*

When called on, stand and answer the question. If you are wrong, a small, red "F'" will be placed next to your name in my roll book. All right, let's begin . . . Judefind, true or false—Baltimore was once capital of the United States?

> JUDEFIND

Uh . . . false?

MR. WINEBURGER

True, true, true, Miss Judefind. You must have been talking on the phone instead of doing your homework last night. It was the capital for two months during the War. That's two red "F's" for you in just one week. It looks like you'll be getting a deficiency!

As the teacher is talking, DAWN pulls a huge meatball sandwich from her purse and begins eating it. A student, MISS HOLLAND, who sits in front of DAWN, is trying to follow the lesson but notices DAWN eating. DAWN gives her threatening looks as MISS HOLLAND raises her hand to snitch.

MR. WINEBURGER
(Noticing MISS HOLLAND'S frantic hand waving)
What is it, Miss Holland?

MISS HOLLAND

Mr. Wineburger, Dawn Davenport is eating a meatball sandwich right out in class! *And* she's been passing notes!

DAWN
(Stuffing the sandwich in her desk)
I was NOT eating.

CONCETTA
(In a loud whisper to MISS HOLLAND)
I got a knife here in my pocketbook and I'm gonna cut you up after class!

MR. WINEBURGER
Stop this immediately!

MISS HOLLAND
(To teacher)
Now they're threatening me, these awful, cheap girls! My mother told me to report this kind of thing, I'm trying to get an education.

MR. WINEBURGER
All of you stop it! Dawn Davenport, stand up!

DAWN stands slowly and defiantly.

"Dawn Davenport is eating a meatball sandwich right out in class!"
(Margie Holland, George Hulse, Susan Walsh, Divine).

MISS HOLLAND
(*Whining*)
I'm *trying* to get an education so I can get into a good college, it's not fair.

MR. WINEBURGER
(*To MISS HOLLAND*)
That will be all. You were quite proper in reporting this incident, but that will be enough.

DAWN
She was trying to copy my homework.

MISS HOLLAND
That's untrue and you know it.

MR. WINEBURGER
Dawn Davenport, you are a habitual liar and I'm quite well aware of it. You will go to detention for a month for this.

DAWN
I won't go—I wasn't eating!

> MR. WINEBURGER
> *(Furiously)*

From your appearance, Miss Davenport, it looks like you never stopped eating!

The whole CLASS laughs cruelly as DAWN becomes more and more embarrassed.

> MR. WINEBURGER
> *(Continuing)*

Get up here!

MR. WINEBURGER drags DAWN to the blackboard at the front of the class.

> MR. WINEBURGER
> *(Continuing)*

Now, write fifty times on this blackboard, "I will not eat in class."

> STUDENT
> *(Yelling out from her seat)*

'Cause I am fat enough already!

DAWN runs from the blackboard and drags the STUDENT from her seat. They begin fighting and pulling each other's hair.

> MR. WINEBURGER
> *(Breaking up the fight and dragging DAWN back to the blackboard by the back of her neck)*

Now start writing and don't stop until I tell you to! I can tell you one thing, Miss Davenport, you can count on a failing grade in Geography this term!

4) Interior public school ladies' room. DAWN, CONCETTA, and CHI-CLET sit on a window ledge ratting and spraying their hair and putting on eye makeup.

> DAWN

I'd like to set fire to this dump.

> CONCETTA

Just 'cause we're pretty, everybody's jealous.

CHICLET
It's like a prison here, even at Christmas it's like a prison.

DAWN
Don't even mention Christmas, Chiclet. My parents are gonna be
real sorry if I don't get them cha-cha heels. I *asked* and I better *get!*

CHICLET
I never get enough Christmas presents, everybody's so damn cheap.

CONCETTA
I should be getting a lot, and I'm gonna take it all back and get the
money for it—you can do that, you know.

CHICLET
We'll probably get caught for hooking this period but who cares!?
Who cares if we fail? It would be fun to be expelled!

DAWN
I hope I get arrested! I hate this school and all these ignorant
teachers who don't know one thing! I'm the one who should be
teaching! I hate my parents too!

5) *Exterior of Dawn's parents' suburban development ranch home. A big
wreath adorns the front door, and the family DOG lies lazily on the lawn.
"Jingle Bells" by Gene Autry plays on the soundtrack.*

6) *Interior knotty-pine family room. Dawn's middle-class parents are
looking through the fancily wrapped presents under the decorated Christmas
tree. MOM and DAD both wear bathrobes and bedroom slippers.*

MOM
(Calling off-screen)
Dawn, come see what Santa brought you!

7) *Interior Dawn's teenage bedroom. She is just waking up. Her hairdo is
wrapped in toilet paper and she wears green baby-doll pajamas.*

DAWN
(Mumbling)
Ah, Christ, I'm comin'.

8) *Interior knotty-pine family room. MOM and DAD sit on the couch.*

MOM
(To DAD)
Please Howard, try to get through this without a fight. I can't stand
another one, not on Christmas.

9) *Interior staircase of Davenport home. DAWN, dressed in same baby-
doll pajamas and fuzzy slippers, is coming down the steps carrying a
wrapped Christmas gift.*

DAWN
(Muttering to herself)
I better get them cha-cha heels.

10) *Interior knotty-pine family room. DAWN enters and hands her parents the gift.*

MOM
How very sweet of you, dear.

DAD
Merry Christmas, honeybunch . . .
(Shaking the present)
Hey, wonder what this is? A fishing rod?

DAWN smirks and sits next to her parents.

MOM
(To DAWN with a big grin)
Won't you join us in a carol before we open our gifts?

DAWN
(Making a face)
Oh, Mother!

DAD
Ah, come on, Dawn. It adds to the spirit.

*They begin singing "Silent Night." DAWN finally relents and joins them
in the last verse of the carol.*

DAWN jumps up and runs over to the tree, selecting an obvious shoe box in bright wrappings. She sits down, squealing with delight and tears off the paper frantically. She suddenly looks horrified and pulls out a pair of Papagallo flat shoes in navy blue.

DAWN
(Yelling at her parents)
WHAT ARE THESE?!

MOM
Those are your new shoes, Dawn.

DAWN
Those aren't the right kind! I told you cha-cha heels—black ones!

DAD
Nice girls don't wear cha-cha heels!

DAWN
(Grabbing parents' presents from their laps)
Gimme those presents! I'll never wear those ugly shoes! I told you the kind I wanted! You've ruined my Christmas!

DAWN throws the presents to the ground and begins stomping on the other gifts under the tree. The crunch of broken glass is heard as she continues to smash gifts. Her parents try to pull her off, completely horrified by her behavior.

MOM
Please, Dawn, not on Christmas!

MOM tries to grab DAWN but DAWN shoves her into the tree. MOM loses balance, tries to steady herself by holding on to the tree, but the tree topples over on top of her, pinning her beneath it. The Christmas balls break but the twinkling lights continue to blink.

DAWN
(To MOM)
Get off me, you ugly witch!

"I better get them cha-cha heels" (Divine, Betty Woods, Roland Hertz).

DAD
(Grabbing DAWN, trying to slap her)
You devil! Come here, you'll pay for this! You devil, Dawn Davenport! Look at your mother under that tree!

Close-up of MOM under the tree. She is weeping and struggling to free herself.

DAWN
(To DAD)
Leave me alone!

DAD
You're such a devil!

DAWN
(Shoving her father to the couch)
Lay off me! I hate you! FUCK YOU! Fuck you both, you awful people! You're not my parents! I hate you, I hate this house and I hate Christmas!

DAWN runs from the room, sobbing.

MOM
(Weeping)
Not on Christmas, not on Christmas!

11) *Exterior Davenport house. DAWN, still in her pajamas, runs out the front door and across the lawn. DAD runs outside and screams after her.*

DAD
Get back in here, Dawn Davenport! You're going to a home for girls, that's where we're going to put you! I'm calling the juvenile authorities right now!

12) *Exterior suburban neighborhood. As "Merry, Merry, Merry Christmas" by Ruby Wright blares on soundtrack, a weeping DAWN runs across a field to a street and begins hitchhiking. EARL, a fat brute, pulls up in an Edsel station wagon on the other side of the street and leers at Dawn. He pulls off, does a U-turn, and stops to pick her up* *

EARL
Get in, sugar dumpling . . .

DAWN hesitates.

EARL
(Continuing)
Come on, honey, hurry up.

13) *Exterior rural garbage dumping area. The Edsel pulls over and EARL and DAWN rush to a filthy, torn mattress and waste no time in preliminaries. EARL begins humping on DAWN.*

DAWN
(Moaning and writhing)
Oh, get it.

EARL pulls down his filthy workpants to reveal torn jockey shorts with "skid marks" on the rear. He again begins brutally humping DAWN.

---

* Divine plays the character of EARL as well as that of DAWN, so we never see their two faces together. A double was used for the male role as Divine plays DAWN, and the double switched to Dawn's costume when Divine played EARL.

EARL
Here it comes! Get ready, get ready!

DAWN
Oh, fuck me, baby, fuck me, that's it!

EARL
Oh, you like that, baby!

DAWN
Oh yeah, yeah, yeah!

While EARL is grunting and pawing, DAWN reaches in his pocket, steals his wallet, and puts it in her imitation leather pocketbook

DAWN
(Continuing)
Eat it! Eat it! Eat it!

EARL begins going down on her as DAWN squeals in passion.

14) *Cut to exterior downtown Baltimore street. DAWN is in an ugly, striped dress, flip-flops, and has her hair in curlers. She is very pregnant. She steps into a pay phone booth, takes out Earl's wallet, looks up his phone number, and dials.*

15) *Interior Earl's metal shop. EARL is hard at work. As he welds at his machine, the phone rings. Aggravated at having to stop his work, he throws off his goggles and waddles over to the phone.*

16) *Exterior phone booth.*

DAWN
(on phone)
Is Earl Peterson there? . . . This is Dawn Davenport . . . DAWN DAVENPORT! You made love to me Christmas morning . . . well, I just wanted to tell you that I'm pregnant, and I want money!

17) *Interior metal shop.*

All knocked up.

EARL
(Fuming into phone)
You stole my wallet, you fat bitch!

DAWN
So what if I did? I want money.

EARL
(Yelling into receiver)
You'll never get any money from me, cow! Just 'cause you got them big udders don't mean you're something special! Get the hook! Go fuck yourself for all I care, YEAH, GO FUCK YOURSELF!

18) Exterior phone booth.

DAWN
(Clicking the button in the phone cradle)
Hello? . . . Hello?

DAWN slams down the handset and walks away from phone booth, holding her stomach.

19) Exterior Albion Hotel. Low-rent Baltimore flophouse.

20) Interior Albion Hotel. Sleazy rented room. DAWN staggers in, falls to the couch holding her stomach, and cries out in labor pains. She takes gum from her mouth, sticks it on the wall, and begins giving birth. DAWN yells and screams in pain and the camera pans down to the NEWBORN INFANT between her legs.

DAWN
(Pulling the NEWBORN INFANT, still attached to
umbilical cord, up to her face lovingly)
Oh, my little Taffy, my little baby Taffy.

DAWN bites through the umbilical cord, spits it onto the wall and hugs the NEWBORN INFANT.

21) Title card. "DAWN DAVENPORT—CAREER GIRL: 1961–1967." "Blue Cat," by Chuck Rio and the Originals, blares on the soundtrack and continues to the end of next title card.

22) *Dissolve to exterior of Little Tavern hamburger shop, a low-rent but iconic Baltimore fast-food restaurant.*

23) *Interior Little Tavern. DAWN, wearing the Little Tavern uniform, sullenly waits on CUSTOMERS. She snatches money from a MALE CUSTOMER's hand and tosses his change back to him.*

24) *Wipe to exterior "Red Garter" go-go bar.*

25) *Interior "Red Garter." DAWN go-go dances on the bar while scabrous OLD MEN whistle and cheer.*

26) *Exterior Baltimore street. "The Block," notorious red-light district. DAWN, CHICLET, and CONCETTA are loitering on a street corner, prostituting themselves. They wear revealing outfits and wave to MEN passing by in cars. A car stops, and they pile in.*

27) *Exterior alley in downtown Baltimore. DAWN, CHICLET, and CONCETTA are hiding behind corner, dressed in black, wearing face masks made out of tulle. A DRUNKEN BUM passes, DAWN, CHICLET, and CONCETTA jump him and steal his wallet and wrist watch.*

28) *Title card. "DAWN DAVENPORT—EARLY CRIMINAL: 1968."*

29) *Dissolve to interior Dawn Davenport's tacky row house. DAWN is reading movie magazines and eating "Texas-style" donuts. Her hair is in curlers, and she wears a black slip and "mystic heel" feather-trimmed gold bedroom slippers. Her daughter, TAFFY, now about eight years old, is wearing an ill-fitting white party dress and is jumping rope.*

> TAFFY
> *(Chanting as she jumps)*
Mabel, Mabel
Set the table!
Don't forget the
Red
Hot
Peppers!

TAFFY begins jumping faster.

DAWN
(Throwing down her magazine is disgust)
Taffy, please stop it! You're giving Mother a migraine.

TAFFY
(Flippantly)
I can jump rope if I feel like it, it's my house too.

DAWN
You can jump rope in the bathroom.

TAFFY
You know it's not big enough in there.

DAWN
Taffy, I have told you repeatedly—no jumping rope within ten feet of me! Those same sing-song rhymes are enough to grate on my nerves.

TAFFY
(Defiantly jumping rope again)
Mabel, Mabel.
Set the table!
Don't forget the
Red
Hot
Peppers!

DAWN
(Clapping her hands for TAFFY to stop)
Taffy, did you hear your mother? Do you want another whipping with that car aerial? It's right in that closet, don't forget.

TAFFY
Maybe I'll stop it and maybe I won't. Why can't I go to school? Why can't I have friends?

DAWN
You can't go to school because I said so! I won't have you nagging me for lunch money and whining for help on your homework. There is no need to know about presidents, wars, numbers, or science. Just listen to me and you'll learn.
(Shaking her finger at TAFFY)

And no little friends over here—repeating rhymes, asking flippant questions, and talking in those nagging baby voices. Can't you just sit here and look out into the air? Isn't that enough? Do you always have to badger me for attention?

TAFFY .
(*Jumping rope and shrieking the chants*)

MABEL, MABEL.
SET THE TABLE . . . !

DAWN
(*Jumping up and grabbing the car aerial*)
Goddamn you! Now, you're going to get it!

TAFFY *begins screaming and running wild throughout the living room, knocking over furniture, smashing vases, spitting and kicking.*

DAWN
(*Trying to smack her with the car aerial*)

I'm going to kill you!!!

CHICLET and CONCETTA *rush in the apartment carrying a TV set and a mink coat. Both are dressed in skin-tight black jeans, heels, low-cut black tops, and have huge hairdos. Both wear their black tulle facemasks.*

CHICLET
(*Removing her mask*)
Hey, Dawn, can we hide this stuff somewhere?

CONCETTA

Hot damn, we got a mink coat!

DAWN
(*Momentarily distracted from TAFFY*)
Sure, girls. Nobody saw you bring that shit in here, did they?

CONCETTA
(*Hiding their loot*)

No, we got it right down the street, nobody was home.

DAWN

Oh, good. Sit down.

(To TAFFY)
You're lucky they came in here, Miss Taffy!

CHICLET
We ought to get ten bucks each just for the TV.

CONCETTA
Hi there, Taffy.

TAFFY *sticks out her tongue.*

DAWN
She's been a hideous little girl today. She was about to get a good whipping.

CHICLET
She looks so cute.

TAFFY
Who are you, ugly?

DAWN
(Disgusted)
You know who they are.

TAFFY
I've never seen them before.

DAWN
Oh, Taffy.

CHICLET
I just saw you yesterday, Taffy.
(Picking her up)
Come sit here with your Aunt Chiclet.

TAFFY *sinks her teeth into Chiclet's arm.*

CHICLET
(Continuing)
Oh, Christ, this kid's biting me!

DAWN
(*Grabbing TAFFY*)
This is the last straw! Help me, Concetta!

DAWN takes Taffy's arms and CONCETTA takes her feet and they carry her up the stairs. TAFFY screams, kicks, and spits the entire way.

CONCETTA
What's the matter with her?

DAWN
She's getting tied to her bed for a week for this!

30) Interior Taffy's dark, dingy bedroom. CHICLET throws TAFFY on the bed and CONCETTA straps Taffy's feet into leg irons while DAWN yanks her arms into overhead handcuffs.

CHICLET
Little piece of shit!

DAWN, CONCETTA, and CHICLET come down the steps as Taffy's screams are heard from her bedroom.

Divine *is* Dawn Davenport.

DAWN

I don't know what I was thinking about when I had her.

CONCETTA

I don't know why you take the shit from her you do, Dawn.

DAWN

I'll never have another one.

CHICLET

Horrible little kid, that goddamn little shit.

31) Interior Dawn's bedroom, a hideously decorated room with a large bed, covered in an ugly purple spread. The walls are painted a glittery black and ridiculous stuffed animals are everywhere. DAWN, CHICLET, and CONCETTA enter and sit on the bed together.

CHICLET

She bit my arm!

DAWN

That child is becoming a monster, you can't imagine—whining and demanding attention and shrieking those same, stupid jump-rope chants day and night! Gimme that jump rope!

CHICLET hands it to her.

DAWN
(Continuing)

Thanks, honey. Give me those scissors.

CONCETTA

Here.

DAWN
(Begins cutting the rope into tiny pieces)

I've had it with this jump rope! That's the last time she's going to jump with the goddamn thing; I hate it!

CONCETTA

I'm glad I had an abortion.

CHICLET
Maybe she needs more punishment.

DAWN
I've done everything a mother can do! I've locked her in room, I've beaten her with a car aerial, *nothing* changes her! It's hard being a loving mother. I giver her free food, a bed, clean underpants—what does she expect? I can't be her little baby friend all the time!

CHICLET
Just get your hair done tomorrow, and you'll feel better. That's what I always do when I get depressed.

DAWN
Maybe I will.

CONCETTA
I tell ya, the Lipstick Beauty Salon is the best. They only let, well . . . you know, special girls in. You have to audition to get your hair done.

CHICLET
And, there's this guy that does hair there—um-um, I'd suck the socks off him in a minute.

CONCETTA
Yeah, Gator's his name. And you know what? He lives right next door!

DAWN
(Getting up off the bed and looking out the window)
Yeah? Wonder what his story is? Maybe he's a chubby chaser!

32) Exterior Dawn's shabby inner-city row house. The camera zooms up to the next-door neighbor's window.

33) Interior of Gator Nelson's row house. Hideous playing-card wallpaper accents an ugly vinyl bar standing in the center of his atrociously decorated living room.

Gator's AUNT IDA enters, wearing a skin-tight, lace-up-the-side leather jumpsuit and five-inch black "Zingy-Zip-Up" spiked heels. She is about fifty years old, has long, bleached hair, and weighs about three hundred pounds. Fat bulges through the lacing on her jumpsuit.

GATOR stands as she enters the room. He wears a cheap "Continental" suit, has long hair and a gold front tooth. AUNT IDA begins posing and wiggling and modeling her new outfit for GATOR.

                         IDA
Ooh-ah-ooh!

                         GATOR
Aunt Ida! Aunt Ida!

                         IDA
You really like it?

                         GATOR
Yeah, all right, Aunt Ida! All right!

                         IDA
                    (Caressing herself)
Oh God! Oooh—ahhh.

                         GATOR
Don't you look hot today!

                         IDA
Why thank you, honey.
          (Caressing herself and gyrating wildly)
I feel more comfortable.

She walks to bar stool and sits down.

                         IDA
                    (Continuing)
Pour me a drink, would ya?

                         GATOR
                    (Going behind her)
Sure, Aunt Ida, what would you like?

                         IDA
Sherry.

Edith Massey and John Waters on set.

GATOR hands her a drink.

> IDA
>
> Have you met any nice boys in the salon?

> GATOR
>
> Some are pretty nice.

> IDA
>
> I meant any nice, *queer* boys. Do you fool around with any of them?

> GATOR
>
> Aunt Ida, you know I dig women.

> IDA
>
> Ah, don't tell me that!

> GATOR
>
> Christ, let's not go through this again.

> IDA
>
> All those beauticians and you don't have any boy dates?

> GATOR
>
> I don't WANT any boy dates.

> IDA
>
> Oh, honey, I'd be so happy if you turned nelly.

> GATOR
>
> Ain't no way! I'm straight! I mean, I like a lot of queers but I don't dig their equipment; I like women.

> IDA
>
> But you could change. Queers are just better. I'd be so proud if you were a fag and had a nice beautician boy-friend—I'd never have to worry.

GATOR
(Laughing)
There ain't nothing to worry about.

IDA
I'd worry that you'd work in an office, have children, celebrate wedding anniversaries. The world of a heterosexual is a sick and boring life!

GATOR
(Shaking his head in disbelief)
Sometimes I think you're fucking crazy. I'm real happy just the way I am.

IDA
(Frantically grabbing him)
Let me bleach your hair out! Let's go down to the Wagon Wheel Bar! I know there's some nice boys there for you.

GATOR
You are fucking nuts, Aunt Ida! I gotta get to work—don't you worry about me, sex ain't no problem.
(Exiting)
See you after my last wash and set.

IDA
(Sadly)
Bye, honey.

IDA shakes her head and guzzles down another glass of sherry.

34) Exterior of the Lipstick Beauty Salon. Blue-collar neighborhood.

35) Interior of the Lipstick Beauty Salon. Everything in the four-chair beauty salon is pastel purple.

Shot of DRIBBLES, a freakish-looking beautician, wildly teasing a customer's hair and insanely laughing.

Shot of WINK, a greaser-type beautician, drinking beer and French-kissing a BLOND CUSTOMER. She is trying to grab his crotch.

BLOND CUSTOMER
Oh, God, I love hairdressers!

Shot of BUTTERFLY, a flamingly gay hairdresser with a huge, blond hairdo, making out with his woman customer.

Shot of GATOR, asleep in his chair, snoring.

Closeup of a flashing red light. A siren goes off and all the beauticians come to military attention next to their customers.

A door marked "Private" opens, and MR. and MRS. DONALD DASHER, the owners of the salon, enter regally. Both are dressed in fancy evening clothes.

DONALD
Good morning, staff, and hello to all the lovely ladies of the Lipstick Beauty Salon.

As the DASHERS walk slowly to the front of the shop, their hairdressers bow to them.

BUTTERFLY
What a beautiful couple.

DONALD
Thanks, Butter.

GATOR
That's a gorgeous outfit, Mrs. Dasher. It must be an original.

DONNA
(Snottily)
It is.

WINK
Bet it cost a fortune.

DONALD
It did.

DRIBBLES
Striking, aren't they? So chic!

DONNA
No kidding.

DONALD and DONNA walk to VIKKI the receptionist's desk. VIKKI, eight months' pregnant, wears a huge hairdo and sports many visible tattoos.

VIKKI
Good morning, Mr. Dasher. You look breathtaking today, Mrs. Dasher.

DONNA
Thank you, Vikki.

VIKKI
There's some applicants for appointments here. Would you like to view them?

DONALD
Anyone particularly appalling?

VIKKI
Well, yes. There is a Dawn Davenport—she seems especially cheap—you may like her.

DONALD
(To HAIRDRESSERS who are still standing at attention)
AT EASE! BACK TO WORK!

HAIRDRESSERS
(In unison)
Yes, Mr. Dasher.

HAIRDRESSERS go back to work.

VIKKI, DONALD, and DONNA walk over to the waiting area where DAWN and three other APPLICANTS for beauty appointments are seated. DAWN wears an orange, see-through dress, and the other APPLI-CANTS are dressed in exaggerated hooker outfits.

VIKKI

All right, girls, line up! Here's your big chance . . . Here they are, Mr. Dasher.

DONALD
(To APPLICANTS)

Back over there so we can see you.

DONNA
(Pointing at APPLICANT A)

Oh my God, look at that one! She's just putrid! You!! Go on, get out!

APPLICANT A looks hurt and confused.

DAWN

You heard her, beat it!

VIKKI

Go on, doll, get out.

APPLICANT A, near tears, runs out of the shop.

DONNA

Forgive me, Donald. I couldn't help it, there has to be a line drawn somewhere.

DONALD

You are quite right, Donna.
(To APPLICANTS B and C)

You see, we are a private salon catering to ravishing beauties only. Even one average customer would be enough to plummet our reputation forever. We must pick and choose with great care . . . Firstly, I'd like to know your occupations.

APPLICANT B

I'm a stripper.

APPLICANT C

And I work for the telephone company.

DONALD

DISQUALIFIED!

VIKKI

I'm sorry, may we suggest Mr. Ray's Wig World?

APPLICANT C

What's the matter with the phone company?

DONNA
(Viciously)
I believe my husband is asking the questions! Go on, GET OUT!
GET OUT OF MY BEAUTY SALON!

APPLICANT C

Well!

VIKKI

Beat it, hon.

APPLICANT C exits.

DONALD
(To DAWN)
And you . . . Miss?

DAWN

Davenport, Dawn Davenport. I'm a thief and a shit-kicker and, uh,
I'd like to be famous.

DONALD
(Smiling in approval)
I see. You're quite striking.

DAWN
(Beaming)
Thank you.

DONALD
(To all APPLICANTS)
We are always curious as to what drew you here to Le Lipstick.

APPLICANT B
Well, I heard all the strippers come here, and I got sick of my old salon.

DONNA
And suppose we become sick of you?

APPLICANT B
(Taken aback)
Well . . . I had hoped that wouldn't happen.

DAWN smiles wickedly.

DONNA
Well, I think it is happening. It's hard to explain, but when I look into your face, I pick up a distinct feeling of nausea.

APPLICANT B
(Starting to get furious)
Hey, wait a minute!

DONALD
DISQUALIFIED! Raising your voice to my wife! In this shop, her wish is my command.

VIKKI
May I suggest Mr. Ray's Wig World?

APPLICANT B
What is she, some kind of princess or something?

DONNA slaps APPLICANT B across the face.

DONNA
(Haughtily)
Princess Perfect!

VIKKI
Hey, get the fuck out!

APPLICANT B
(Exiting)
The Better Business Bureau will be hearing from me!

DONNA
(To APPLICANT B)
Just get out!
(To BEAUTICIANS)
ATTENTION!

Once again, the BEAUTICIANS snap to attention.

Close-up of DONALD and DAWN.

DONALD
Staff . . . this is our new customer, Miss Dawn Davenport.
(To DAWN)
This is Dribbles . . . Wink . . . Gator and Butterfly.

DAWN
(To DONALD)
I'd like to have Gator if it would be alright.

DONALD
Certainly.
(To GATOR)
Gator, see to it that Miss Davenport is well taken care of.

DAWN runs to Gator's chair and jumps in, giggling and smiling.

DAWN
. . . Oh, Gator, I've heard so much about you. Could somebody run
and get me a double egg salad on white toast?

GATOR
Certainly, Dawn.

DAWN
(Squealing in delight)

Oh, good!

*36) Exterior picturesque street in Fells Point area. GATOR and DAWN
are walking hand in hand by the harbor as the instrumental "Yogi," by
Bill Black, is heard on soundtrack.*

DAWN and GATOR stop to window-shop in front of cheap bridal salon.

Close-up of mannequin in bridal gown.

*DAWN snuggles up to GATOR and looks back to bridal mannequin in
window.*

*37) Interior church. "Bridal March" performed by 101 Strings plays on
soundtrack as DAWN and GATOR walk down the aisle with their only
bridesmaid, TAFFY. DAWN wears a see-through white wedding gown;
even her pubic hair is visible. GATOR is dressed in a fake tiger-skin
tuxedo and TAFFY wears another fancy party dress.*

Gator (Michael Potter) and Dawn wed.

Entire STAFF of the Lipstick Beauty Salon is in church, dressed in their gaudiest outfits. AUNT IDA, dressed all in black, is weeping and shaking her fist in the last pew.

PRIEST says the wedding vows and pronounces GATOR and DAWN husband and wife.

CONCETTA and CHICLET wipe tears of joy from their eyes.

38) Exterior church. All the GUESTS throw rice at GATOR and DAWN. AUNT IDA rushes from the church, shoves DAWN, and attacks the PRIEST, knocking off his hat and shoving him to the ground as the surprised GUESTS try to restrain her.

39) Title card. "DAWN DAVENPORT—MARRIED LIFE: 1969." "Underwater," by the Frogmen, blares on the soundtrack and continues until next title card.

40) Interior Dawn's living room. Night. DAWN, dressed in lingerie, is tapping her feet impatiently and furiously smoking a cigarette. GATOR enters drunk, tries to paw DAWN, and she begins hitting him with a rolling pin.

41) Interior Dawn's living room, days later. DAWN, returns home carrying groceries and hears erotic sounds coming from her bedroom.

42) Interior Dawn's bedroom. A NUDE YOUNG WOMAN is sitting on Gator's face. He is also nude. DAWN throws down the bag of groceries and starts smacking them both.

43) Exterior Ida's house. Backyard. IDA is dumping her garbage onto Dawn's lawn, next door. When DAWN leans out her window to protest, IDA gives DAWN the finger.

44) Exterior front of Ida's house. Later. IDA comes out her front door dressed in her leathers and sashays up the street, oblivious to the outside world. We see DAWN watching from the second floor of her house. As IDA passes beneath Dawn's window, DAWN throws down a large, dead mackerel and hits IDA on the head with it.

45) Title card. "DAWN DAVENPORT—FIVE YEARS LATER: 1974."

46) *Interior Dawn's bedroom. GATOR is humping DAWN, at the same time reading a copy of* Popular Mechanics. *His opened tool box lies nearby on the bed.*

> DAWN
> *(Nearing orgasm)*
> Oh . . . oh . . . oh! Can't you put down those damn magazines?!

> GATOR
> *(Breathing heavily)*
> I like these damn magazines!

> DAWN
> Better than me, I suppose!

> GATOR
> Nope, just about the same in my book.

> DAWN
> *(Panting)*
> Can't we do normal?

> GATOR
> This is normal.

> DAWN
> Ah . . . oh! Oh!!

> GATOR
> Give me my tool kit!

> DAWN
> Get it yourself.

GATOR, still on top of her, pulls his tool kit over from the other side of the bed and takes a hammer from it. He begins rubbing it on her body.

> GATOR
> Feel like a hammer today, Dawn?

DAWN
(*Moaning*)
No, not the hammer, Gator! Use the needle nose pliers!

GATOR takes a pair of needle-nose pliers from his tool kit.

GATOR
You asked for it, baby!

DAWN is in ecstasy as GATOR starts fucking DAWN with the needle nose pliers.

TAFFY DAVENPORT, now aged fourteen*, enters the room. She wears a ridiculous child's dress and makeup that makes her mouth and eyes seem crooked.

TAFFY
(*Disgustedly*)
God, look at you two! Caught right in the act! Isn't that a pretty sight!

DAWN and GATOR jump up and cover themselves.

DAWN
Taffy, GO TO YOUR ROOM!

GATOR
Hey, Taffy baby, cool down. Come on over here with your daddy.

DAWN
(*To GATOR*)
Don't talk to her like that.

TAFFY
You're not my daddy, you disgusting hippy pig! I wouldn't get near a bed that had been defiled by the likes of you two—I'd sooner jump in a river of snot!

---

* Now played by twenty-six year old Mink Stole.

DAWN

Well, go jump then. Go kill yourself and do us all a favor.

Close-up of Gator's cock.

GATOR

Hey Taffy, baby, come suck your daddy's dick.

TAFFY

I wouldn't suck your lousy dick if I was suffocating and there was oxygen in your balls.

DAWN

You pay some respect, Miss Taffy! And if I catch you spying and nosing around here one more time, I'm going to put you in the mental hospital.

GATOR

She can't help it, she's retarded.

TAFFY

I AM NOT RETARDED!!

DAWN

Oh yes you are, Taffy. I had you tested when you were a little girl. A staff of doctors examined you and maybe the reason you don't remember is that they told me you are most definitely retarded.

TAFFY

I never went to any hospital! That is a rotten, filthy lie!

DAWN

I'm afraid it's the truth. I don't like it any better than you do. To think that my genes were polluted by your birth is not a very pleasant thought.

TAFFY

Oh, how can I call you my mother? I wish I had been an orphan.

GATOR

You can tell she's retarded. Look at her face—she has the face of an old woman.

DAWN

It's true. Look in the mirror, Taffy. For fourteen, you don't look so good. It's because you've been such a brat all your life that now all that brattishness is showing on your face; the face of a retarded brat.

GATOR

Yessiree, that's a real time-warp of a face you've got there.

DAWN
(Elbowing GATOR)

What do you know about anything? Some of the faces I've seen you with could stop a train.

TAFFY

Give me ten dollars!

DAWN

Awfully demanding, aren't you?

TAFFY

Give me ten dollars or I'm calling the police. Don't think I'd hesitate to put you two slobs behind bars for the rest of your life.

GATOR

What would you do with ten dollars?

TAFFY
(To GATOR)

Writing a book, hippy? Why don't you go listen to some folk music and give me a break?

DAWN
(Laughing at Gator's embarrassment)

Taffy Davenport!
(To GATOR)
Give her the money.

GATOR

What?!

DAWN

You heard me, I said give her the ten dollars!

GATOR takes out a bill and TAFFY snatches it from his hand. She exits the bedroom and obnoxiously stomps up the steps to her bedroom as loudly as possible.

GATOR and DAWN are, once again, thrashing and moaning on the bed. Dawn's eyes are closed and her mouth is wide open.

GATOR

You diggin' it, baby?

DAWN

Oh Gator! Gator! Gator!

GATOR reaches under the bed and gets a large carrot. DAWN is still moaning and GATOR shoves the carrot into her mouth and jumps off the bed laughing.

DAWN
(Choking and yanking the carrot from her mouth)
Real funny, Gator!!

GATOR
(Laughing)
You should have seen your face!

DAWN

I've had it with you! Why don't you just GET OUT? Go back to your fat aunt and leave me alone.

GATOR

I got off on it, I really got off on it!

DAWN
(Testily)
Oh, did you? Well, hip, hip, hooray for your cheap climax!

What about me, fuck-face? Some pitiful excuse for a husband you turned out to be. Why don't you just go take your fucking tool kit and go fuck a garage?
> *(Fixing her hair in the mirror)*
I'm going to go get my hair done.

> GATOR

I couldn't help it. If you could have seen the expression on your face ... I thought I'd piss myself when I saw that carrot in your mouth.
> *(Grabbing the carrot and trying to rub it on DAWN)*
It's a weird joint, ain't it?

GATOR laughs.

> DAWN

You're cut off for two weeks for this! And don't, just don't, even bother to speak to me at the salon, either. Just pretend we don't know one another!

47) *Interior of the Lipstick Beauty Salon. CHICLET and CONCETTA are both having their hair done. SALLY, a large, glamorous woman, occupies another chair and is chatting with the beauticians.*

VIKKI hands a CUSTOMER her bill at the desk. The customer has a huge, freshly-done hairdo.

> VIKKI

That will be a hundred and four dollars, please.

> CUSTOMER

For a wash and set?

> VIKKI

Well, I don't know what you're accustomed to in good grooming but this *is* the Lipstick Beauty Salon, and not some bargain-basement beauty school.

> CUSTOMER

That's outrageous. I won't pay that for a wash and set.

VIKKI
Give us back the hairdo, then.

CUSTOMER
What are you talking about?

VIKKI
(Yelling to the beauticians)
Boys, she won't pay! Take the hairdo back!

BUTTERFLY, DRIBBLES, and WINK throw down their brushes and combs and menacingly approach the frightened customer.

BUTTERFLY
What do you mean, she won't pay?

WINK
Wait 'til I get my hands on her.

The BEAUTICIANS grab the CUSTOMER mess up her hairdo, dump a vase of flowers and water on her head, and shove her out the door.

VIKKI
I oughta rip her face off!

WINK
She had a hell of a lot of nerve.

The BEAUTICIANS return to their customers. DRIBBLES begins combing his customer Sally's hair.

DRIBBLES
Sorry for the interruption, Sally. You're one of my prettiest customers.

SALLY
Oh shut up, Dribbles.
(Feeling her hairdo)
The things a woman has to go through to get some height.

DRIBBLES
How's your little girl? Why don't you bring her in here more often?

SALLY
Why? So you can undress her with your eyes? For Christ's sake, she's only six years old.

DRIBBLES
I know, but I just like to play with her. I wish I was a little girl.

SALLY
Well, throw a goddamn penny in a fountain and make a goddamn wish and maybe it will come true.

CONCETTA and CHICLET are getting their hair done by WINK and BUTTERFLY.

CONCETTA
(To CHICLET)
So, I told her, you can keep your fuckin' ten dollars. I can steal ten dollars faster than they can make it.

CHICLET
What's the big deal about money? It's so easy to get, I can't imagine why anyone works. It boggles my imagination.

BUTTERFLY
(To CHICLET)
Maybe everybody's not a common thief like you.

CONCETTA
Butterfly, you tired thing, we are anything but common . . .

WINK
I love the smell of shampoo . . .

CHICLET
(To BUTTERFLY)
We are upper-echelon cat burglars and don't you forget it, Mr. Butterfly!

> WINK

. . . Of course I think I like the smell of Clairol Creme conditioner better, you know, when it's on a freshly bleached head. I don't know . . . I like them both but . . .

> CONCETTA
> *(Interrupting WINK)*

Oh, shut up.

> BUTTERFLY

Don't pay them any mind, Wink. They wouldn't know beauty if they fell over it.

DAWN *enters the salon in a black see-through cocktail dress and sunglasses.*

> VIKKI

Oh, hi, Dawn.

> DAWN
> *(Holding back tears)*

Good morning, Vikki. I'd like my hair done quickly and quietly.

> VIKKI

Sure, hon. You want Gator? Is he here today? You want him to do it?

> DAWN

No, I don't Vikki, and if you must know, I'm thinking of a divorce. So, please don't ever mention his name to me again.

> VIKKI

I'm sorry to hear that, Dawn. Is Gator coming in today?

> DAWN
> *(Sobbing)*

I'm really not aware of his schedule. Please . . .

> VIKKI

I'm sorry, honey. I know what you're going through, I really do. But they're all bastards! Cheer up—you don't need him.

DAWN
Just get somebody to set my hair, please.

VIKKI
Okay, hon.

Phone rings at reception desk.

VIKKI
(Continuing)
Excuse me a minute, hon.
(Answering)
Hello . . . why yes, she's right here . . . Why certainly.
(Hanging up, excitedly)
That was Mr. Dasher, Dawn! He wants to see you in private! No one has ever been back there before; it must be something big!

DAWN walks through the salon to the Dashers' private entrance in the rear.

DAWN
Hi, Sally. Hi, Concetta.

SALLY
Hi.

WINK
Hi, Dawn.

DAWN
Hey, Wink.

CONCETTA
Hi, Dawn, how are you?

DAWN
Listen, I can't talk to you now. I gotta go see Mr. Dasher.

CONCETTA
Oooohhh!

                              BUTTERFLY
See you later, hon.

                              DRIBBLES
   Bye.

DAWN knocks at the Dashers' private door.

                              DONALD
   Come in.

48) Exterior Dashers' apartment. DAWN enters down a long hallway.

                              DONALD
   In here.

*DAWN enters the Dashers' ridiculously formal parlor. Both of the
DASHERS are very dressed up.*

                              DAWN
   Oh . . .

                              DONALD
   Good to see you, Dawn.

                              DAWN
   Hello, Mr. Dasher.

They all sit down.

                              DONNA
                    *(Drinking out of a goblet and offering DAWN the
                    same glass)*
   Sip of soda?

                              DAWN
   Oh . . . thank you . . .
                    (Taking a sip and handing it back to DONNA)
   . . . I don't understand this honor.

DONALD
You will in time, Miss Davenport . . . My wife and I, and please do
call us Donald and Donna, are wondering if you wouldn't be interested in becoming involved in show business?

DAWN
(Eyes lighting up)
SHOW BUSINESS?!

DONNA
Well . . . sort of show business. You see, Dawn, we're planning a
little experiment, a beauty experiment you could call it, and we
want you to be our model . . .

DONALD
. . . Sort of a glamorous guinea pig, you might say.

DAWN
A . . . beauty experiment?

DONNA
My husband and I enjoy taking pictures a great deal and we'd like
you to pose for some rather unusual shots.

DAWN
Oh . . . do you mean pornography?

DONALD
(Offended)
Certainly not! Sex is not one of our interests. As a matter of fact,
one of the rules you must always obey is to never, ever mention the
sex act in front of us.

DONNA
We find the subject most repellent. We must ask that you observe
this rule at all times. You should know that we view sex as a violation of the spirit, and we would certainly never allow ourselves to
be caught in one of those ludicrous positions.

DAWN
(Trying to be polite)
Oh . . . of course, of course. I'm so sorry . . . I really didn't know.

DONALD
Are you still a thief, Dawn?

DAWN
Yes, I am! Not as much as I used to be, but I still rob houses.

DONNA
With those other two?

DAWN
Yes, Chiclet and Concetta.

DONALD
Would you allow us to take some photos of you committing various crimes; crimes that tickled our fancy?

DAWN
I . . . I guess so.

DONNA
You see, our experiment involves beauty and crime; we feel them to be one.

DONALD
We have a theory that crime enhances one's beauty; the worse the crime gets, the more ravishing one becomes. We want you to prove us right.

DONNA
Say yes, Dawn! Aren't you sick of getting your hair done? Don't you want the throbbing excitement of a modeling career? We'll give you a new look, an interest in life, and together we can overcome this boredom that imprisons us all.

DAWN
I'd love to have the two of you take my photos, but I won't get arrested, will I?

DONALD

The police department will not be involved.

DONNA

And any special favors . . . well, don't hesitate to ask.

DAWN

There . . . is one thing.

DONALD

Ask and you shall receive.

DAWN

Fire my husband!

DONALD

Gator?

DAWN

Yes, I want a divorce!

DONALD
(Picking up phone and dialing the receptionist)
. . . Vikki? . . . This is Mr. Dasher . . . Please fire Gator . . . No
reason . . . Yes, tell him no reason at all.

DAWN *giggles.*

*49) Interior of beauty shop. GATOR is waiting for DAWN, and he is
furious. The other OPERATORS pretend to work but are all gossiping
about GATOR and DAWN.*

BUTTERFLY

Trouble's coming up now.

*DAWN exits the Dashers' apartment and walks through the salon,
ignoring GATOR.*

GATOR

Hey, fatso, I want to talk to you.

> DAWN
> *(Turning her nose up)*
Just speak to my attorney.

> GATOR
Hey, did you get me fired?

> DAWN
Maybe I did, and maybe I didn't!

50) Exterior Lipstick Beauty Salon.

> DAWN
> *(Exiting and yelling over her shoulder to Gator, still inside)*
SHUT UP!

51) Interior Dawn's living room. TAFFY is seated on the couch. Set up in front of her is a broken car windshield with a dummy's head through it, a steering wheel, and lots of broken glass. TAFFY squirts ketchup on the dummy and pretends she is driving a car.

> TAFFY
> *(Screaming)*
Aaahhhh! Look out!

TAFFY covers her face and falls back as if she has been in a terrible accident.

DAWN enters.

> DAWN
How many times have I told you to play car accident outside?

> TAFFY
> *(Squirting ketchup on herself)*
Ooh mother, it was a terrible accident!
> *(Pointing to dummy)*
Look at my friend—she was in the death seat and her head got caught in the windshield! The ambulance should be here soon, I think. I'm okay . . . I guess . . . It wasn't my fault! The other car came out of nowhere! I slammed on the brakes but . . .

Taffy (Mink Stole) plays "car accident."

DAWN
LOOK AT THIS MESS, TAFFY! Broken glass and ketchup all over
my fine furniture!

TAFFY
(Still playing, sobbing)
Call another ambulance! Call anybody! HELP ME!

DAWN
Where did you get this crap, Taffy? I told you to spend that money
I gave you on a cute outfit but oooh-nooo! As soon as my back is
turned you run right out and spend it on props for your morbid
little games. Well, I want it cleaned up pronto! We're having guests
for dinner, and I want you in tip-top behavior and looking as P-R-
E-T-T-Y as humanly possible.

TAFFY
(Suddenly snapping back to reality)
WHO'S COMING TO DINNER?!

DAWN

Donald and Donna Dasher are going to join us for a small, informal buffet, and if you dare to embarrass me in front of them . . .

TAFFY

If I have to eat with Gator, I'll spit food!

DAWN

I'm afraid I'm going to have to be the one to break the news to you, Taffy. I've thrown Gator out and started divorce proceedings. I don't want to seem overly bitter but I'd appreciate it if you'd destroy all of his belongings!

TAFFY

Well, hal-le-lu-yah! I'd be happy to, mother.

DAWN
(Walking up the stairs to second floor and pausing)
I'm going to go sink into a long, hot beauty bath now and try to erase the stink of a five-year marriage. Someone at such a tender age as you, Taffy, might find it difficult to understand what a long, hard painful decision this was on my part. I'm a free woman now and my life is just ready to begin.

52) Interior of Ida's house. IDA sits chatting with her friend, ERNIE. IDA wears a tight party dress, and ERNIE is dressed very effeminately.

IDA
(Offering ERNIE a bowl of pretzels)
Oh, Ernie, have another pretzel for Chrissake. Wait 'til you meet my little Gator—you two are going to fall right in love.

ERNIE

My dear, I hope so. Are you sure he's gay?

IDA

Well, I just use common sense—if they're smart they're queer, and if they're stupid they're straight. Right, Ernie? Are you sure you won't have another pretzel?

ERNIE

I'm sure, Miss Thing, I'm sure. Pretzels give you plaque.

GATOR enters.

GATOR

Hello, Aunt Ida.

IDA

Gator, what a coincidence. There's somebody here dying to meet you. Ernie, this is Gator. Gator, this is Ernie.

ERNIE

Hi, stud.

GATOR
(Disgustedly)

Get him out of here!

Ernie (Bob Adams) and Aunt Ida (Edith Massey).

IDA

Gator Nelson, you be polite to Ernie! He wants a date with you.

GATOR

Well, I don't want a date with him! I came to say good-bye, Aunt Ida. I'm moving to Detroit.

IDA

WHAT?!

GATOR

I want to be near the auto industry. I'm sick of hairdressing and, besides, Dawn had me fired.

ERNIE

I can get you a job in the baths, Mary.

GATOR

Look, fucker, take a walk, alright?

ERNIE

Well!

GATOR

Look, you better beat it before I punch your fucking face out the window.

ERNIE

(To IDA)

No "gay knocks" for me, Ida. At best, all you've got is trade.

IDA

Oh, Gator, Ernie's your type! Move back in with me and we'll get you a job as a female impersonator.

ERNIE

(To IDA)

His hands are too big, darling . . .

(To GATOR)

Bye, Gator.

> *(Blowing him a kiss)*
> It was fab meeting you.

GATOR

Fuck you!

ERNIE exits.

IDA

You can't leave!

GATOR

Well, I am.

IDA

Oh, Gator, I'm sorry about Ernie. I thought you'd be cute together. Anybody's better than Dawn Slobenport.

GATOR

I'll be alright, Aunt Ida. I'm just sick of everything here. I'm going to Detroit to find happiness within the auto industry.

IDA
> *(Falling to her knees and clutching onto Gator's coat)*
> No, Gator, no! I'll die if you leave! No Gator! Please don't go!

GATOR

You'll be alright. Good-bye, Aunt Ida.

GATOR exits. IDA falls to the floor and begins having a fit; pulling her hair out, rolling around the floor, and foaming at the mouth.

IDA

No! No! Gator! No! Ahhhhhh! NO! NO! NO!

53) Exterior Dawn's house. GATOR approaches and knocks on front door.

TAFFY
> *(Answering the door)*
> WHAT??!!

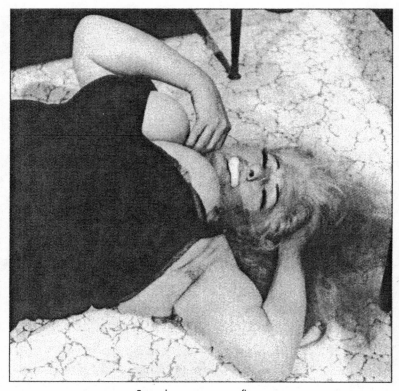

From the cutting room floor.

GATOR

Hi, brat. Is your mother home? I've got a little going-away present for her.

TAFFY
(Yelling into the house)
Hey, mother, there's a shithead here to see you.

DAWN
(Coming to the door)
What are you doing on my porch? I told you not to come moping around here anymore.

GATOR

Don't have so many hard feelings, Dawn. I brought you a little present to remember me by.

DAWN

Yeah? What is it?

GATOR punches DAWN in the mouth, knocking her unconscious to the floor.

54) Exterior Dawn and Ida's street. DONALD and DONNA DASHER stroll down this slum alley looking for Dawn's house. DONALD has his camera around his neck.

DONNA

God, this neighborhood's hideous. I'm scared rats are going to come out and bite my new nylons.

DONALD

True, it's not Beverly Hills, but crime breeds in these neighborhoods, Donna. It's really an oh-so-perfect place for our crime model to live; I rather like it.

DONNA

I'm glad I didn't wear one of my designer originals. The air's so sooty and damp, our clothes will be ready for the Goodwill after this.

DONALD

Stop being so prissy, Donna. Excitement is not always clean. You must get used to this low life, for here lies beauty—crime and beauty.
     (Stopping in front of Dawn's house)
Oh, here it is—how perfect!

55) Interior Dawn's house. Knocking is heard at the front door. DAWN comes out from kitchen to answer the door in a purple-jeweled dress. She has a nasty black eye.

                    DAWN
Hold on. I'll be right there . . .
            (Letting the DASHERS in)
Hi . . . come on in.

                    DONALD
Good evening, Dawn.

                    DONNA
Hello.

                    DAWN
Hi . . . Did you have any trouble finding the place?

                    DONALD
The directions were pinpoint perfect and your street . . . well, it's a
street of charm.

                    DAWN
Oh, thank you.

                    DONNA
            (Looking around)
Lovely! And I bet you cleaned just for us.

                    DAWN
I did tidy up.

                    DONALD
Uh . . . What happened to your eye?

                    DAWN
Oh, that . . . I'm so embarrassed. I fell getting on the bus and hit
my eye right on the farebox. Well, I felt like a damned fool.

                    DONALD
May I take a photo of it?

                    DAWN
            (Posing)
Certainly.

DONALD takes the photo.

DONNA

Nice!

DAWN

I love having my picture taken. Oh, I'm sorry, sit down.

They enter the living room and sit down. The coffee table has been set for dinner, and baskets of chips and pretzels are also on the table.

DAWN
(Continuing)
I'm so excited about having you come here for dinner.

DONALD

That's a stunning arrangement.

DAWN

Thank you. You both look so nice.

TAFFY stomps in the room wearing a ballerina outfit and ridiculous ribbons in her hair. Her makeup is smeared and more crooked than ever.

DAWN
(Embarrassed)
I'd like you to meet my daughter, Taffy. Taffy, this is Mr. and Mrs. Dasher—they're going to put Mother in show business.

TAFFY

Is the circus in town?

DAWN
(To DASHERS)
She's SO funny. If you'll excuse me, I'll go check on dinner. Help yourself to the chips.

DAWN exits to kitchen.

TAFFY sits next to the DASHERS who slide away from her in discomfort.

                    TAFFY
What's that camera for?

                    DONALD
To take pictures of your mother.

                    TAFFY
HER!??

                    DONALD
We happen to think she's quite beautiful.

                    TAFFY
You must be cockeyed then!
            *(Thrusting the bowl of chips on DONNA and spilling
            half of them on her)*
Hey, lady, want some chips?

                    DONNA
            (Daintily picking the chips off)
Really . . . I couldn't. Thanks, but . . . uh, no thanks.

                    TAFFY
            (Mimicking her voice)
Thanks but no thanks!

DAWN enters the room wearing an apron.

                    DAWN
            (To DASHERS)
Do you want your spaghetti with or without cheese?

                    DONNA
I'll have two chicken breasts, please.

                    DAWN
            (Embarrassed)
Well . . . uh . . . we're not having that, we're having spaghetti.

                    DONNA
I couldn't possibly eat spaghetti. Do I look Italian?

DONALD

We rarely eat any form of noodle, Dawn, but I'll take a tiny portion to be polite. With cheese, please.

DONNA

I'll have an extremely large glass of ice water.

TAFFY

I want mine with lots of cheese!

DAWN
(To TAFFY, testily)
I'm afraid there's not enough for you, Taffy. How about some toast?

TAFFY

WHAT DO YOU MEAN THERE IS NOT ENOUGH?!! You can feed these two hambones, and you can't feed your own daughter?

DAWN

Taffy, don't make me lose my temper in front of company!

DONALD snaps a photo of DAWN. DAWN smiles and fixes her hair.

DAWN
(Back to TAFFY)
Now, there's not enough food for you to eat. Perhaps if Mr. Dasher leaves some on his plate, you may have first picks, but I can NOT be running out to the supermarket just for you!

TAFFY

If I can't have any, nobody can!

TAFFY runs into the kitchen.

DAWN
(Alarmed)
You come out of that kitchen!

TAFFY
(Running back into living room holding pot of
spaghetti)
They can't have it, and I want it!

DAWN
Put that food down, you little brat!

TAFFY
I won't!

DAWN
You lay off that food, you horrible little brat. I paid for that food!

TAFFY lets out a blood-curdling scream and throws the pot of spaghetti
at the wall. The bowl shatters and spaghetti is all over the wallpaper and
furniture.

DAWN
(Continuing)
OH MY GOD!
(Picking up a chair to hit TAFFY)
I'M GOING TO KILL YOU!

DAWN hesitates so DONALD can take her photo and then smashes
TAFFY over the head with the chair. The chair splinters into pieces and
TAFFY is knocked unconscious. DONALD takes another photo.

DONNA
This is so exciting! Just think of all the little horror stories that go
on in other people's lives.

DONALD
(To DAWN)
Your dinner party has been a smashing success!

DAWN
I'm so sorry you had to be a witness to all this. I didn't want to tell
you but my daughter is retarded. A child psychologist told me to
beat her unmercifully whenever she acted up, but it's never gone
this far. I hope she's not . . . dead!

DONALD
(Taking more photographs of Taffy's body)
These photographs will be stunning! How about a few more
quickie shots if you don't mind.

DAWN
(Eagerly posing)
Anything for you, Donald.

DONALD
(Looking through lens)
Ah! Look rough!

DAWN strikes a mean pose.

DONNA
Look happy!

DAWN smiles wildly.

"A smashing success" (Divine, Mink Stole, Mary Vivian Pearce, David Lochary).

DAWN
I love those flashbulbs!

DONALD
Look horrified at what you've done to your daughter.

DAWN poses in mock terror.

DONALD
(Continuing)
Look like you've just won a prize.

DAWN clasps her hands over her head and puts one foot on Taffy's stomach.

DONNA
Great!

56) *Exterior Dawn's and Ida's houses. IDA runs from her house to Dawn's, screaming and ranting.*

IDA
Dawn . . . you son of a bitch!

57) *Interior Dawn's house. DAWN is still posing for the DASHERS. IDA pushes her way into the house and starts screaming at DAWN.*

IDA
You! You're the one who did it! You drove Gator away!

DONALD
(Snapping Ida's photo)
Oh my God!

DONNA
Incredible!

DAWN
Ida Nelson, you get out of my house!

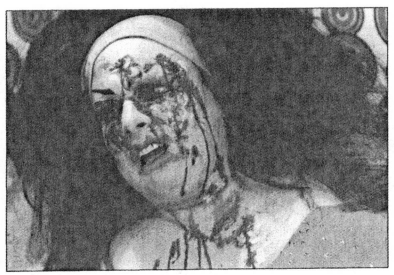

"Acid! Acid!"

IDA

You made Gator leave!
(Taking a vial of acid from her pocket)
I've got something for your face, motherfucker!

IDA throws the acid in Dawn's face and exits.

DAWN
(Screaming in pain and covering her bleeding face)
AAAAHHHH! God! God!

DONNA
(Excitedly)
Acid! Acid! It's eating her face!

DONALD
(Getting his camera focused on DAWN who has staggered over to the couch)
Move, Donna. These will be the most exquisite shots yet!
(To DAWN)
Hold still while I focus! Move your hands!

> DAWN
> *(Her face bleeding profusely and barely able to speak)*
Help me.

> DONNA
Operation Excitement is off to a flying start!

> DONALD
> *(Taking pictures)*
Just one more shot, Dawn. You are beautiful.

Close-up of Dawn's mangled face.

> DAWN
> *(Weakly)*
Thank you, Mr. Dasher.

58) *Interior hospital room. DAWN is in hospital bed, her face entirely covered in bandages.*

59) *Interior hospital corridor. CONCETTA, CHICLET, WINK, BUT-TERFLY, and DRIBBLES are waiting to visit DAWN. DONALD and DONNA are nearby, talking with a DOCTOR. DONALD, as always, wears his camera around his neck.*

> DONALD
So what you are saying, Doctor, is that even though there is no hope for the scar tissue to develop, makeup, in itself, would not be harmful to the patient.

> DOCTOR
> *(Appalled)*
Well . . . I suppose not, but I find it most peculiar you would even discuss makeup. What she needs is a good plastic surgeon.

> DONNA
Nonsense, Doctor. With proper makeup treatments her scars will be mere beauty marks.

> DONALD
The medical profession has always shown its extreme ignorance in

"Morally bankrupt" (Eddie Dixon, Susan Walsh, Cookie Mueller, Paul Swift, George Figgs).

the beauty field. What you don't realize, Doctor, and really how could you, is that Miss Davenport will now be more beautiful than if she had had a million-dollar face-lift.

DOCTOR

What I find most distasteful is the fact you've chosen to bring a camera. Her face has been hideously disfigured; certainly this is no time for photographs.

DONNA

Why not let us worry about proper timing?

DONALD

Yes, why don't you mind your own business.

DOCTOR
(Enraged)

In all of my years in the medical profession, NEVER have I encountered such a morally bankrupt group of people! Why, not only are you selfish and vicious . . .

CHICLET, CONCETTA, WINK, BUTTERFLY, and DRIBBLES laugh.

> DOCTOR
> *(Continuing)*
> . . . but you have no feeling for the cares of your loved ones. And my BILL will reflect your attitude in this hospital.

DONALD snaps a photo of the DOCTOR.

> DONALD
>
> Gorgeous!

> DOCTOR
> *(Trying to grab Donald's camera)*
> Why, you gaudy little . . .

> DONALD
>
> Uh, uh, uh. Watch it, Doc; I sue and bruise easily.

A NURSE enters the hall.

> NURSE
> Miss Davenport is ready for her guests.

> DONNA
> *(To DOCTOR)*
> See you in malpractice court.

60) Interior Dawn's hospital room. The NURSE enters, followed by the DASHERS, CONCETTA, CHICLET, BUTTERFLY, WINK, and DRIBBLES, all carrying presents.

> NURSE
> Dawn, your friends are here.

DAWN tries to mumble through the bandages and waves.

> CONCETTA
>
> Hi, Dawn.

DAWN
(Barely audible)
Hello, everyone.

DONALD
Hello, Miss Beautiful. We're all here for the unveiling. It's like a holiday for us.

DONNA
This is so exciting! Let's all say "hi."

CHICLET
Hi, Dawn. It's me, Chiclet. I can't wait to see your new face, I hear it's stunning.

CONCETTA
It's Concetta, Dawn. I'm so jealous . . . Everyone tells me you're the prettiest now.

DRIBBLES
Dribbles, here. I hope that fart of a doctor hasn't been giving you any trouble.

WINK
It's Wink. I can't wait to do your hair, doll.

DAWN
Oh, thank you, honey. Thanks to everyone!

BUTTERFLY
It's Butter, baby. You'll be a goddess with this new face, a goddess of gore to protect all of your children in crime.

DAWN
I want to see it . . .
(Groping in the air with her hands)
Nurse . . . nurse! Remove my bandage.

NURSE
(Beginning to unwrap the gauze)
She asked me to remind you that she is, of course, without makeup.

BUTTERFLY

That's all right.

WINK

We understand.

DONNA

Don't worry about makeup, Dawn.

DONALD
(Focusing his camera)
Slowly, nurse, slowly. I want perfect focus.

CONCETTA

I can smell flesh! God, I could faint, I'm so excited.

CHICLET

It's just like an art opening!

DRIBBLES

Christ, I wish it had happened to me.

BUTTERFLY

Just think of how it would look with *my* hair.

WINK

I'm getting a hard-on. Beauty always gives me a hard-on.

DONNA
(Horrified)
Aim it the other way, then, Wink. You know how I detest organs!
Beauty has absolutely nothing to do with . . . that word . . . that
thing you have there hanging like an obscene pickle. Spare me your
anatomy!

NURSE
*(Removing the last bandage of Dawn's hideously
scarred face)*
There it is; one hell of a rotten face!

ALL

Ooh! Ahh! Ooh! Ahh!

BUTTERFLY

Beautiful!

DONALD

Gorgeous, gorgeous, gorgeous.

DONNA

It makes the Mona Lisa look like a number painting.

CHICLET

Acid does what Eterna 27 cannot!

CONCETTA

Your face for the world to see!

DRIBBLES

Breathtakingly beautiful!

WINK

Give her a mirror— let her see the miracle!

BUTTERFLY
(Handing DAWN a mirror)

Beauty, beauty, look at you. I wish to God I had it too.

DAWN slowly takes the mirror and looks at herself. Horrified at the hideous scars, she recoils in disgust. Everyone applauds, and DAWN nervously smiles.

DAWN

Pretty, pretty?

ALL
(Applauding)

Yeah!

"Pretty, pretty?"

                    DONALD
              (Handing DAWN a gift)
Look what we brought you.

DAWN opens the present to reveal a silver lamé hostess outfit.

                    DAWN
Oh, Donald, it's beautiful.

                    DONNA
        (Handing DAWN a huge basket of cosmetics)
And look at all this makeup we have for you. You're so stunning
. . . I could cry in the face of beauty.

                    DAWN
        (Looking uncertainly at her face again in the mirror)
You . . . really like it?

                    ALL
Oh, yes!

                    DAWN
I guess . . . I kind of do, too.
              (To DONNA)
Would you put my makeup on for me?

DONNA

I'd love to, Dawn.

WINK

Isn't that sweet?

DONALD

Nothing is too good for our crime model.

DAWN

Oh, thank you, Donald.

61) Interior Dawn's completely remodeled house. Everything is red glitter: the floor, the walls, even the drapes. A little stage with curtains is at one end of the living room and a huge, wrapped birthday present is at the other. Enter DONALD, DONNA, and DAWN. DAWN is dressed in her new hostess outfit, has had her hair done, and wears grotesque makeup in an unsuccessful attempt to hide the scars on her face.

DAWN
(Shocked at the new decorations)

Oh!

DONALD

Surprise!

DONNA

How do you like it, Dawn?

DAWN

Oh, Donna . . . it's beautiful!

DONALD

All the time you were in the hospital recovering, we were busy; busy trying to make you happy!

DONNA
(Handing DAWN a bill)
Here's a hundred dollars, too.
(Handing her another wrapped gift)
Here's something else for you to treasure.

DAWN
(Opening it)
Oh, what is it?

A portrait taken by DONALD of Dawn's bleeding face from the acid-throwing party is revealed.

DAWN
(Continuing)
Oh . . . a portrait! You're both so good to me! Ever since I met you my life's been like a vacation. Oh, look, a little stage!

DAWN runs to stage, jumps up on it, and starts wildly modeling.

DONALD
Specially built, Dawn, all for you. All for the model of the year.

DONNA
We've been hoping for a rather insane camera session.

DAWN
(Mugging hideously for the camera and insanely waving her arms about)
Come on, I'm ready! I'm just in the mood for a red, hot camera session!

DONALD
(Taking photos)
Slowly, Dawn, slowly. You'll give me a heart attack.
(Taking a syringe out of his jacket pocket)
Let me give you some . . . medicine.

DAWN
(Puzzled)
What kind, Donald? Is it . . . a beauty treatment?

DONNA
Yes, Dawn, exactly. It's eyeliner. Liquid eyeliner.

DONALD
We cooked it down this morning. It won't hurt . . . nothing hurts. Have you ever mainlined?

> DAWN

No, but I will . . .

DONNA puts a belt around Dawn's upper arm and DONALD brings the needle nearer.

> DAWN
> *(Continuing)*

. . . Keep taking those pictures, and I'll do it . . . Come on, SHOOT ME!

> DONALD
> *(Plunging the needle into her arm and forcing the black liquid through the needle)*

Feel it in your blood? Caressing your corpuscles—the wonders of liquid eyeliner! Say it! Say "liquid eyeliner!"

> DAWN

LIQUID EYELINER!

DONALD takes the needle out of her arm and DAWN begins to go completely berserk in her "modeling."

> DONNA
> *(Aroused)*

Give us something twisted! Give us something warped!

DONALD takes photos and DAWN struts and poses obscenely on the stage.

> DAWN

I'm glad I met you! I love crime too—especially the excitement of getting away with it!!

> DONALD

These photos will be art.

> DONNA

Hard-core art!

> DAWN

You ain't seen nothing yet! I'll model for eternity for you. Just let me hear the click of that camera.

DONALD snaps a photo.

> DAWN
> *(Clutching her crotch)*

Oh! Ah! Oh! Just think of it—house robbing, new gowns, murder, scars, fingerprints, LASHES!!!

DONNA faints from excitement.

> DONALD
> *(To DONNA)*

Wake up, you're missing the best part. She hasn't received all of her gifts yet.

> DONNA
> *(Slowly coming to)*

Beauty? . . . eyeliner? . . . Oh, forgive me Donald, it was really just too much for me . . .

> DAWN
> *(Frantically)*

WHAT PRESENT? GIMME ANOTHER PRESENT!

They all run over to the huge gift.

> DONALD

Here's your biggest surprise yet.

> DONNA

Open it! For God's sake, open it!

> DAWN
> *(Ripping off the paper)*

It's as big as a house . . .

Inside the wrapping paper is a huge, ornate birdcage. In the cage, tied and gagged, is IDA, dressed in a white feather dress.

DAWN
(Horrified)
Oh my Christ, IT'S HER!

DONALD
Specially kidnapped for your amusement.

DONNA
With no ransom, of course.

DONALD
She's so beautiful, we figured you'd want to keep her here, caged like a rare bird.

DAWN
Beautiful!? You mean she has to live here, in my own home?

DONALD
Only for a temporary period, until we've gotten all the photos we need for our experiment.

DAWN
But . . . she disfigured me!

DONNA
She did you a favor and now you can return the favor.

DONALD
(Handing her an axe)
Cut off the hand that threw the acid!

DAWN
(Looking at IDA pitilessly)
Whatever you say, Donald!

DONALD *forces Ida's hand through the bars of the cage onto a cutting block.*

DAWN
(Continuing)
Ida Nelson, I'm going to chop off your scrawny, little paw!

DONALD
(Fumbling with his camera)
Hold it . . . look excited . . . ACTION!

DAWN chops Ida's hand off.

Closeup of hand being severed.

Closeup of the bloody stump.

Closeup of the severed hand on the floor.

DAWN
(Wildly modeling)
How was that for a beauty photo, Mr. Donald Dasher? Get those
cameras rolling!

Shot of IDA, unconscious in the cage.

DONALD
(Taking lots of photos)
Great! Great!

*TAFFY suddenly enters the living room. DONALD kicks the severed
hand under the couch to hide it from TAFFY.*

TAFFY
WHAT'S GOING ON IN HERE?!

DAWN
(Trying to pretend that everything is normal)
Oh . . . oh . . . why, hello, Taffy . . . did you miss Mommy? I'm
home from the hospital, I'm alright.

TAFFY
I was hoping the next time I saw you would be at your funeral. You
sure look ugly!

DAWN
Not everyone seems to feel that way.

DONALD
(Trying to be casual)
Donna, I think it's time we were going. It's been a long day, and I'm feeling a bit damp.

DONNA
Ditto, Donald. I really should be changing my outfit anyway. I've had it on nearly five hours.

DAWN
(To the DASHERS)
I want to thank you both again for everything.

DONALD
Our pleasure. Would you care to join us for dinner tonight?

DAWN
Why, I'd love to.

DONNA
Light dinner—you may want to eat before you come.

TAFFY
Am I invited?

DONALD
N! Good afternoon.

DAWN
Bye.

DONNA
Bye.

DAWN
Thanks again.

The DASHERS exit.

TAFFY
Why didn't you send money while you were away? How was I sup-posed to eat?

DAWN

Come, come, Taffy. It doesn't look like you starved to death, does it?

TAFFY

I want to leave here.

DAWN

Well, good riddance to bad rubbish.

TAFFY

What are you trying to do to me?! Why are you always with those people?!
(Eyeing IDA)
Why is *she* in that cage?

DAWN

I'm modeling for the Dashers, that's all. And Ida, well, she's our new pet. You always wanted a pet, Taffy—I thought you'd be pleased.

TAFFY

You're trying to drive me crazy, aren't you? I can't stand it anymore!
(Pleading)
Mother . . . please, tell me—who is my real father?

DAWN

I told you never to ask me about that! If it was up to him, you'd be rotting in some foster home.

TAFFY

I don't care! I've got to know! Tell me!

DAWN

Oh, very well—go see him. He hates you anyway.

TAFFY

Where does he live? What's his name?

DAWN

If you must know, his name is Earl Peterson. I haven't seen him in
a decade, Taffy. I may have his address stored on a piece of paper
in an old shoe in my bureau—I really can't remember.

TAFFY exits to the bedroom.

*62) Exterior country dirt road. A nervous TAFFY walks through mud
puddles, clutching a piece of paper containing the address of her father.
She wears a stupid-looking pink child's dress.*

*63) Interior slum. EARL PETERSON, in filthy work clothes, is drunk in
front of a TV. He is partially bald now and his house is a mess. A boar's
head is stuffed and mounted on the wall.*

*64) Exterior country dirt road. TAFFY finds Earl's house, hesitates nerv-
ously, and knocks on the door.*

TAFFY

Daddy? Daddy? It's me, Taffy!

65) Interior slum. EARL looks puzzled and throws down an empty beer can.

EARL

I don't know nobody named Taffy! I'm busy right now.

66) Exterior slum. TAFFY knocks harder.

TAFFY

Oh, please let me in, daddy. Open the door!

67) Interior slum. EARL gets up and staggers to the door.

EARL

Ah, fucking shut up! Alright, already!

*EARL opens the door and TAFFY leaps up on him, hands around his neck
and feet around his waist. EARL staggers backwards.*

TAFFY

Daddy—it's me, Taffy—your long, lost little girl!

EARL
(Pushing her off of him)
Hey, get off! I ain't your daddy, I ain't even married.

TAFFY
Oh, I know that, but you're my daddy alright. My mother told me.
My mother is Dawn Davenport.

EARL
I don't know nobody named Dawn Darlinport.

TAFFY
Oh, but you must! Mother told me! Please! Let me stay with you
awhile.

EARL
(Thinking)
Yeah . . . You can stay here awhile . . . want a drink?

EARL begins guzzling from a pint of liquor.

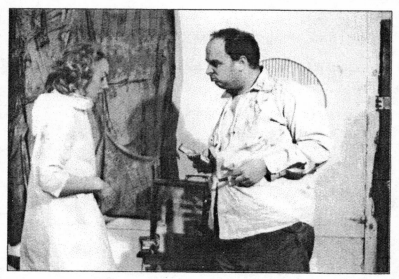

Taffy meets Daddy Earl (Mink Stole, Divine).

TAFFY
NO! You don't even believe me, do you?

EARL
Yeah, yeah. Hey, I'll be your sugar daddy, how about that?
(Belching loudly in Taffy's face)
I'm feelin' a little drunk so don't mind me.

TAFFY
Shitface! You're my father—doesn't that mean anything to you?

EARL
Who'd you say your mother was?

TAFFY
Dawn Davenport. You know her.

EARL
What does she look like?

TAFFY
Fat. Very fat.

Shot of stuffed, wild boar on wall.

EARL
Yeah, yeah . . . I maybe remember.

TAFFY
(Trying to hug him)
Oh daddy, I knew you would. Mother's been awful to me. For
years, I've suffered. Please let me stay with you. I won't be any
trouble. I'll help you clean and we can go out together and maybe
. . . maybe you could buy me some regular clothes . . .

EARL
Can you fuck as good as your mother?

TAFFY
(Slapping EARL across the face)
PIG! You goddamn slimy pig!

EARL tries to grab TAFFY.

                         EARL
    Hey little Taffy, can you stretch like Taffy?

                         TAFFY
                       (Struggling)
    Fuck you.

TAFFY accidentally knocks Earl's liquor bottle to the floor.

                         EARL
    Hey, you spilled my drink!
              (Pulling out his syphilitic penis)
    Daddy Earl's got a little present for you . . .

*TAFFY weeps uncontrollably. EARL begins gagging and vomits on
TAFFY.*

                         EARL
                      (Continuing)
    I'm sorry . . . I been drinking.

EARL collapses in his chair.

Close-up of a butcher knife in an opened, filthy mayonnaise jar.

*TAFFY grabs the knife and beings stabbing EARL in the chest. Blood
splatters on Taffy's clothes as she continues stabbing and weeping.*

TAFFY throws the knife down and runs from the house.

*68) Exterior crowded downtown Baltimore street. DAWN, now wearing
an aqua, leopard-print dress, with one arm completely covered over with
fabric looking like a claw, "models" her way up the street as astonished
PASSERSBY turn to gawk at her exhibitionism.*

*Close-up of MALE staring at DAWN as she "models" by him. His glass
eye pops out of its socket.*

69) Interior Dashers' house. DONALD and DONNA sit on an ornate bed in evening clothes, looking through some of the photographs they have taken of DAWN.

> DONALD
> *(Pointing to one)*
> I like this one best, it has little Taffy in it.

> DONNA
> *(Laughing)*
> I bet the police would love to get their hands on these.

70) Exterior Lipstick Beauty Salon. DAWN "models" up to the front door and knocks at the Dashers' private entrance.

71) Interior Dashers' apartment.

> DONALD
> Come right on in, Dawn.

DAWN, wildly posing, enters.

> DAWN
> Hi.

> DONNA
> Evening. Don't you look pretty.

> DAWN
> Oh, thank you.

> DONNA
> Subtle out, isn't it?

> DAWN
> Well . . . it's beautiful. And God, my walk over here was fabulous. Everyone was staring and gawking at me like a princess.

> DONALD
> Naturally.

They all sit down.

> DONALD
> *(Continuing)*
> We all know you're beautiful. It just takes the stupid little world a little longer to catch on—always has.

> DONNA
> *(To DAWN)*
> And, don't forget the influence of that medicine we gave you. Eyeliner taken internally heightens one's beauty awareness.

> DAWN
> Believe me, I realize that now. I had never felt complete until I had experienced an eyeliner rush.

> DONALD
> We've been on the stuff for months. Doctors and other simpletons may frown upon it, but we beauty czars know what is good for the blood.

> DONNA
> Would you like to shoot some more? I had some orally earlier.

> DAWN
> No . . . no thanks, Donna. I'm still up on it now.

> DONNA
> *(Handing her a plate of mascara brushes, daintily displayed on lettuce)*
> Would you like an hors d'oeuvre, then?

> DONALD
> Eat one. They're really quite tasty.

> DAWN
> Oh . . . little mascara brushes!

DAWN takes one and eats it, chewing it uncertainly, and choking a little. With difficulty, she swallows it.

DONNA

Yummy, huh?

DAWN

... Yes ... delicious ... but where's your camera?

DONALD

It's here, don't worry about that. We have lots of important business matters to discuss. We've decided that the time is ripe for you to blast off into show business.

DAWN
(Wiggling in her chair)

I'm ready, Mr. Dasher.

72) Interior Dawn's living room. TAFFY sits weeping in the corner. IDA is now conscious and on her stump, replacing her hand, is a mean-looking hook.

IDA
(To TAFFY)

You little bitch! Let me out of this goddamn bird cage.

TAFFY

Little bitch? Is that all the thanks I get? I got you the hook, didn't I? Mother will kill me as it is.

IDA
(Shaking her hook at TAFFY)

Who cares about your stinking mother? She stole my Gator away but she ain't gonna get me! And I'll thank you for this fucking hook after I rip her eyes out with it! Gimme something to eat.

TAFFY

There's no food here. Mother doesn't buy food for me. You want an egg? There might be a couple old eggs in the kitchen.

IDA

NO, I don't want no goddamn eggs! I want meat and potatoes!

TAFFY
(Sobbing)
Please don't yell at me. I've had a horrible experience today. I can't help what's happened to you any more than I can help . . . what I did today. Don't you think I hate mother as much as you do?

IDA
Let me out of this cage, little Taffy, and I'll give you a cookie!

TAFFY
I can't let you out yet. I promise I will but I need time to think. I don't have any place to go . . .
(Suddenly)
Maybe I could go live with those Hare Krishna people! They're always nice to me when I see them downtown. Maybe . . . maybe I could help them out. I just want something nice to happen in my life! If only I could go live with the Krishnas—they'd help me!

DAWN enters. She has shaved her head except for some teased curls on the crown and is not pleased to see that TAFFY is back.

DAWN
What are YOU doing here? I thought you went to live with your father.

TAFFY
(Nervously)
He moved . . . he wasn't at that address.

DAWN
Pity, pity.
(Seeing IDA)
Who un-gagged this maggot?

TAFFY
You told me she was my pet. I was just playing with her.

IDA
You let me out of here, Dawn Pigport, or you'll be sorry!

DAWN

Now, now, now, Ida. You're supposed to be singing a sweet little song. Are you hungry? The Dashers sent some crackers for you—Ida want a cracker?

IDA
(Trying to smack DAWN with her hook)
Fuck off!

DAWN
(Seeing the hook)
Who gave you that hook?!
(To TAFFY)
Was it you, Taffy?

TAFFY
(Trembling)
No, I swear.

DAWN

Oh, yes it was, you sneaking conniving little abortion!

TAFFY
(Pleading)
She was in pain.

DAWN

You're a pain too, Taffy—a pain in my big asshole.

IDA

I'll see you fry in the electric chair for this! I'll personally see that you fry in the goddamn chair for this.

DAWN
(Advancing towards the cage)
I'll shut you up! Where's that gag?

IDA

Fucker! Pig fucker!

DAWN
(Trying to gag her with rag)
What's that, a mating call? I'll shut that big flytrap.

IDA
Hetero! Filthy hetero stink shit!

DAWN
(Successfully gagging IDA and slamming cage door)
You'll never get out of here now, and I won't clean your cage for a week.

TAFFY
You're insane. My own mother is insane.

DAWN
(To TAFFY)
You stop that fake blubbering and don't go getting any crocodile tears on my new furniture either.

TAFFY
Look at you! You're a freak! My God, what's happened to your hair?

DAWN
Haven't you ever heard of style, Taffy?

TAFFY
(Defiantly)
I'm going to live with the Hare Krishna people!

DAWN
WHAT DID YOU SAY?!

TAFFY
The Krishnas are love, mother.

DAWN
God. I would have killed you at birth had I thought you would even entertain such an idea.

TAFFY
(Chanting)
Hare Krishna! Hare Krishna!

DAWN
Stop that bullshit! Where did you meet those awful people? Are they trying to brainwash you? Can't you see how pretty your mother is? Don't you envy me? Do you want to walk around the streets, dressed in rags, selling STINK STICKS?

TAFFY
Incense, mother, incense . . . Hare Krishna! Hare Krishna!

DAWN
STOP THOSE CHANTS! You're just trying to get on my nerves, now. I would die of embarrassment if you ever dared link my name with that pack of fools. Think of my career! Why . . . I'd sooner you be a secretary.

TAFFY
(Chanting louder)
HARE KRISHNA! HARE KRISHNA! RAMA HARE KRISHNA!

DAWN
(Grabbing TAFFY)
I'm warning you right now, Taffy. If I'm ever downtown and see you dressed in one of those ridiculous outfits, bothering shoppers and dancing around like some sort of fool . . . I'LL KILL YOU! And I mean business!

TAFFY
You can't kill love, mother. You can't kill Krishna because Krishna is consciousness.

DAWN
(Gagging)
Oh God!

TAFFY
Hare Rama! Hare Rama!

DAWN
(Shaking her finger)
I'll show you consciousness when I knock you unconscious! Taffy, I have a busy week ahead of me—I have hours of studying to do on my new nightclub act. If you feel you must stay here, I ask you to constantly remember that you ARE in the presence of a star!

TAFFY
OOMMMMMMM!

DAWN
(Exiting)
Jesus Christ Almighty!

73) *Exterior Superstar Nightclub. A poster announces "Dawn Davenport—In Person. Free Makeup." A long line of YOUNG PEOPLE wait to enter the theater. DRIBBLES and WINK collect tickets and bark the show.*

WINK
Step right up ladies and gentlemen! Right this way!

DRIBBLES
Free makeup in the lobby!

WINK
See the most beautiful woman alive!

DRIBBLES
You'll get the surprise of your lives!

WINK
This is a show you will not believe!

74) *Interior Dawn's backstage dressing room. DAWN applies the final touches to her outrageously heavy eye makeup that reaches all the way around to the back of her shaved head. What's left of her hair is teased into a monstrously high peak. DONALD and DONNA are taking photos while CHICLET and CONCETTA give DAWN moral support.*

CONCETTA

You should see the crowds out there, Dawn! It's packed.

CHICLET

God, you'll be a household word overnight.

CONCETTA

Just think—flashbulbs popping, your picture in the paper, writers in the audience, artists just begging to paint you. It's just like you were president!

DONNA

Tonight she'll be even more important than the president.

DAWN

I just can't wait to get out there! I can feel exhibitionism throbbing in my veins!

75) *Interior Dawn's living room. IDA is still in the birdcage. TAFFY enters dressed in complete Krishna outfit. A sandle paste Tilaka mark is on her forehead, her nose is pierced, and she carries finger cymbals.*

IDA

Where have you been, Taffy? I thought you left me here to rot.

TAFFY

I'm living with the Krishna people now, Ida. I've finally found my inner peace.
(*Showing her a key*)
I'm going to set you free now.

IDA
(*Overjoyed*)
Oh, thank Christ, Taffy. Quick, honey, let me out. My ass hurts from this stool. If you let me out right away, I'll buy five dollars' worth of incense from you.

TAFFY
(*Freeing her*)
All this time you've been in this cage you could have been meditating—why, you're practically in the lotus position right now.

IDA
(Climbing out of the cage)
Thank you! Thank you!

TAFFY
I want you to go immediately to the police department. Tell them my mother, the enemy of spirituality, is at Superstar Nightclub, and I want her arrested tonight. Tell the police everything.

IDA
I'll go right to the police station, Miss Taffy, and I'll report it all. And remember, my offer still stands—if you get tired of being a Hare Krishna, you come live with me and be a lesbian.

TAFFY
Fly away! Fly away quickly, like a little bird! Tell the police, His Divine Grace, the Bhaktivedanta Swami Prabhupada has spoken!

IDA
(Exiting)
Thank you, Taffy. I will. I will.

76) Interior Superstar Nightclub. Packed AUDIENCE stomping their feet and clapping for the show to begin.

77) Interior Dawn's dressing room. DAWN is posing wildly with a gun while DONALD snaps photos. CHICLET, CONCETTA, and DONNA shout encouragement.

DONALD
(To DAWN)
Give us the violent beauty!

DAWN continues posing and then falls to her knees and prays.

DAWN
Oh, Richard Speck, guide me through this night. Help me to be brave on this night of glamour!

DAWN leaps from her knees and "models" again, squealing like a pig.

TAFFY barges into the dressing room in her Krishna outfit.

TAFFY

Hare Krishna, mother.

DAWN
(Furiously)
You've finally done it, haven't you? Embarrassed me on my night
of fame! No reporters saw you, did they?
(Turning her head in disgust)
Look at you! I could vomit.

TAFFY

I thought I'd come and see you one last time before your karma
caught up with you. Mother, it's not too late—come to the temple
with me!

DAWN gags.

DONALD

The exact opposite of beauty!

DONNA

Remember Alice Crimmins.

TAFFY

All of you—can't you see what you're doing?—worshipping the
flesh and ignoring the spiritual. If only you could see the light! Dis-
covering my consciousness was like finding a million dollars in the
street. I'm glowing with happiness!

DAWN

Well, glow on, Miss Taffy, because the sight of you makes my flesh
crawl. I'm sick of listening to you babble commandments and
spout gibberish! It's turning my stomach, do you hear? In just a few
seconds I'm going to put you out of your happiness!

TAFFY
(Bellowing the chant as obnoxiously as possible)
HARE KRISHNA, HARE KRISHNA, HARE KRISHNA!

                              DAWN
        SHUT UP!

                              TAFFY
                HARE RAMA . . . HARE RAMA.

                              DAWN
        SHUT UP!

DAWN lunges for TAFFY and begins strangling her as DONALD,
DONNA, CHICLET, and CONCETTA cheer her on.

                              DAWN
                          (Continuing)
                SHUT UP! SHUT UP! SHUT UP!

Taffy's eyes bulge and she collapses on the floor, dead.

                              DAWN
                          (Laughing)
        She's finally dead!
                          (To DONALD)
        I think I'm ready to go on now.

78) Interior Superstar Nightclub. AUDIENCE cheers.

Shot of a large trampoline in the center of the stage.

DONALD DASHER comes from backstage to stage center.

                              DONALD
        Attention! Ladies and gentlemen, I'd like to introduce the most
        beautiful woman in the world—the fabulous DAWN DAVENPORT.

DONALD exits to wild cheering.

DAWN comes onstage dressed in a jeweled, white jumpsuit with artificial
hair used as fringe. She goose-walks around the trampoline, obscenely
groping herself.

DAWN gets on the trampoline and does a knee-drop, a frontal drop, and
a back drop.

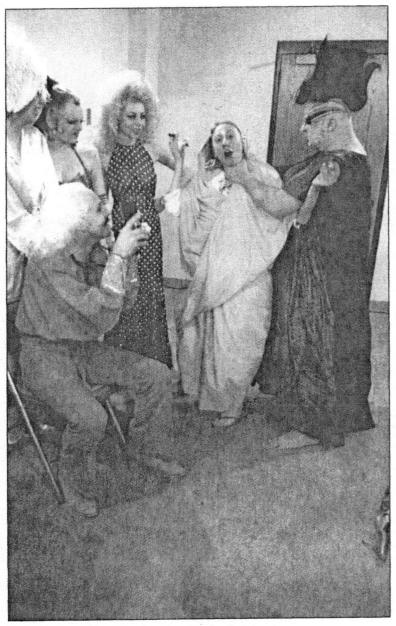

Dawn Davenport murders her daughter.

On the trampoline.

AUDIENCE goes wild.

DAWN does a back flip.

AUDIENCE cheers in amazement.

DAWN jumps off the trampoline and again rushes around the stage, gyrating obscenely.

DAWN rips a phone book in half and flexes her muscles.

DAWN jumps into a kettle of fish and rubs the fish over her body. She throws one of the fish into the AUDIENCE.

CHICLET and CONCETTA applaud wildly and smear makeup on their faces.

DAWN grabs a gun and rubs it between her legs. She takes the gun and begins licking and sucking it. She fires the gun over her head.

The AUDIENCE is silent.

DAWN

Thank you! I love you! Thank you! Thank you from the bottom of my black, little heart! You came here for some excitement tonight and that's just what you're going to get! Take a good look at me because I'm going to be on the front page of every newspaper in this country tomorrow! You're looking at crime personified and don't you forget it! I framed Leslie Bacon! I called the heroin hotline on Abbie Hoffman! I bought the gun Bremer used to shoot Wallace! I had an affair with Juan Corona! I BLEW RICHARD SPECK! AND I'M SO FUCKING BEAUTIFUL I CAN'T STAND IT MYSELF!!

AUDIENCE cheers wildly.

DAWN shoots the gun over her head again.

DAWN
(Aiming suddenly at the AUDIENCE)
Now everybody freeze! Who wants to be famous? Who wants to die for art?

"Who wants to die for art?"

MEMBER OF AUDIENCE
(*Standing up, smiling, thinking it's a joke*)
I do!

DAWN *shoots him in the stomach. The* AUDIENCE *panics and begins stampeding for the door.* DAWN *fires wildly into the* AUDIENCE, *killing a few more* SPECTATORS. PEOPLE *are trampled and injured in the mad race for the exits.*

The POLICE *arrive, charging into the riot.* DAWN *runs out the exit and escapes. The* POLICE *fire into the crowd, killing a few more members of the* AUDIENCE *including* BUTTERFLY, WINK, *and* DRIBBLES.

79) *Exterior Superstar Nightclub. Scared members of the* AUDIENCE *run into the street in panic.*

DONALD *and* DONNA *run out, but they are grabbed by a burly* POLICEMAN *with a gun.*

POLICEMAN
(*To* DASHERS)
Freeze before I blow the bleach-blond head off ya!

DONALD *and* DONNA *put their hands in the air.*

DONNA
We surrender! We're innocent. She went berserk, she was on drugs.

DONALD
(*Weeping*)
Don't shoot us! We're clean, please don't shoot us.

80) *Exterior woods. Rain, sleet.* DAWN *comes out of pup tent still dressed in rain-soaked theatrical jumpsuit and brushes her teeth with her finger from water in a stream. She hears* DOGS *barking in the distance and runs away in fear.* TWO COPS *run through the woods with barking* DOGS, *firing pistols in the air.*

COP A
Come on out, Davenport!

COP B

We've got you this time, Davenport. There's no way out. You haven't got a chance.

DAWN runs through woods in a panic.

Another COP with a DOG stops.

COP C
(To COP A and COP B)
You go that way—I'll go this way!

81) Exterior raging river. The rain has turned to sleet. DAWN jumps in and swims across the freezing rapids without messing up her hair. As DAWN reaches the shore, COP A and COP B rush toward her.

COP A

Freeze, Davenport.

COP B
(Arresting DAWN)
Put your hands behind your back!

DAWN
(Struggling)
I didn't do one thing!

82) Interior of a criminal courtroom. The JURY is present as is the JUDGE. At one table sits Dawn's Ivy League-ish DEFENSE ATTORNEY and at the other sits the prosecutor, MR. WILROY.

DAWN, wearing a prison uniform with handcuffs and shackles and sporting an exaggerated Mohican haircut, is led by two, burly MATRONS into the courtroom and to her lawyer's table.

DAWN
(To MATRONS)
Get off! You pigs!!

JUDGE
(Banging the gavel)
Court is now in session.
(Looking toward prosecutor)
Mr. Wilroy—

MR. WILROY
(To JUDGE)
Thank you, your honor.
(To the COURT)
Your honor, defense counsel, ladies and gentlemen of the jury: the case we have before us is one of the most savage crimes ever perpetrated by one individual in the history of the state of Maryland. The evidence will prove beyond a reasonable doubt that the defendant, Dawn Davenport . . .

DAWN laughs.

MR. WILROY
(Continuing)
. . . is guilty of not only kidnapping but first-degree murder. Her victims came from all walks of life: young people, an elderly woman, police officers, and even the defendant's own daughter. It is a sordid and sickening case that can end in only one just verdict—guilty! I ask you to show the defendant the same mercy she showed her victims—sentence her to die in the electric chair.

Dissolve to MR. WILROY questioning IDA NELSON on the stand. IDA has had her hair done and wears a flashy cocktail dress.

MR. WILROY
. . . Let's go to the night of April 22nd. Do you remember that night?

.
IDA
(Looking right at DAWN)
Yes, I do!
(To MR. WILROY)
I was at home, having some sherry and listening to records when Dawn Davenport came to my door and pulled a gun on me!

Dawn in court with her attorney (Mumme, Divine, Chris Mason, Seymour Avigdor).

DAWN
(Held back by MATRONS at defense table)
That's a lie, Ida Nelson!

JUDGE
(Banging on the gavel)
Order! Order in this courtroom!

IDA
It's the truth, Pigport, and you know it!! She forced me at gunpoint into her crummy little house, stripped me of my clothes, and forced me to exhibit myself in front of her.

DAWN
You liar! LIAR!

                    IDA
She made me put on a feather dress, locked me in a birdcage and . . .
                (Holding up her hook)
. . . cut of my arm with an axe!

              DEFENSE ATTORNEY
I object, your honor, on the grounds that this witness is not com-
petent and that she is senile.

                    JUDGE
Overruled.

Dissolve to MR. WILROY.

                MR. WILROY
I call to the stand Donna Dasher.

*DAWN looks to back of courtroom, hoping to see DONNA. DONNA
enters wearing a conservative suit and hat.*

                    DAWN
            (To her DEFENSE ATTORNEY)
She'll tell the truth.

DONNA pauses to give DAWN a cold glare.

                    DAWN
                (To DONNA)
Hi, Donna! We all know about excitement, don't we?

              DEFENSE ATTORNEY
Shhh!

                    DAWN
        (To DONNA as she approaches the stand)
The press is all here, and I'm looking real pretty, but these two
witches won't give me my fashion accessories.

The MATRONS quiet her.

JUDGE

Order in this courtroom!

(Turning to DONNA)

Now, Mrs. Dasher, you understand that you have been granted total immunity for your testimony?

DAWN looks horrified.

DONNA

Yes, thank you, your honor. It is *total* immunity?

JUDGE

(Smiling)

Yes, Mrs. Dasher, total.

MR. WILROY

You became involved taking pictures of the defendant, is that correct, Mrs. Dasher?

DONNA

Yes, fashion photographs.

MR. WILROY

Could you tell us a little about these "photography sessions?"

DONNA

They never really amounted to much, Mr. Wilroy. We soon learned that Dawn's modeling abilities were rather limited. She would pose and strut all the time, as if she thought we enjoyed the sight of such sickening exhibitionism. She even scarred her own face in order to attract attention. She would talk of nothing but crime and criminal behavior and she even seemed to idolize Richard Speck . . .

The JURY MEMBERS shake their heads in disgust.

MR. WILROY

Anything else, Mrs. Dasher?

DONNA

One time she . . .

> MR. WILROY

Go on—go on.

> DONNA

She used a needle in front of me! I was shocked silly but said nothing, hoping that maybe she was diabetic and hadn't told me. Then, all by accident, we discovered she had kidnapped the woman next door!

DAWN lunges from her seat and the MATRONS drag her back to the table.

> DAWN

You lying bitch! You're the one that gave me those beauty treatments! You're the one who kidnapped Ida! You lying, bleached-blond bitch! LIAR! LIAR!

Dissolve to MR. WILROY questioning DONALD DASHER on the stand. DONALD wears a suit and tie.

> MR. WILROY

Could you tell us about the evening of May 8th?

> DONALD

Yes, that is the night we went to what Miss Davenport refers to as her "nightclub act." We were backstage, Dawn was wild-eyed, pacing up and down, ranting and raving about her beauty when in reality she looked . . . quite hideous.

DAWN is now gagged in the courtroom.

> DONALD
> (Continuing)

Her daughter, Taffy, came in and they had a big fight over religious freedom. Donna and I were terrified but stood by, helplessly. The fighting continued and Dawn strangled her daughter to death right in front of us.

DAWN struggles to yell behind from behind her gag.

MR. WILROY

What happened then?

DONALD

She ran onstage to begin her so-called act; a pitiful display based solely on how disgusting she could be. She seemed to work herself into a frenzy, shouting ridiculous claims of criminal conduct, grimacing wildly into the audience and then, before we realized it, she pulled a gun out and began shooting into the crowd.
(Sobbing)
I can't describe the horror! It was nothing but screams and panic—I lived through hell that night.

Dissolve to DEFENSE ATTORNEY addressing the court.

DEFENSE ATTORNEY

Your honor, Mr. Wilroy, ladies and gentlemen of the jury we have heard a lot of witnesses condemn my client. We have heard some incredibly bizarre testimony and we have seen some damaging physical evidence. But, my client is innocent. Innocent by reason of insanity! Listen to her testimony, listen to the whispering of a madwoman and decide for yourselves. If she is not insane, who is? I do not ask you to forgive her, I do not ask you to set her free, I ask you to have the courage to help her. Find her insane so she can be put away in a mental hospital for the rest of her natural life.

Dissolve to DAWN being questioned on the stand by her DEFENSE ATTORNEY.

DEFENSE ATTORNEY
(Continuing)
Dawn, how did you become acquainted with Donald and Donna Dasher?

DAWN

I . . . I went to their beauty parlor and they discovered me. I was so beautiful! I still am the top model in the country.

JURY bursts out laughing.

DAWN

(Continuing)

I don't want my trial to be held here! I want it to be downtown in a large, large theater where I belong.

(Whispering to her DEFENSE ATTORNEY)

You're a terrible press agent, they won't even let cameras in here.

DEFENSE ATTORNEY

I'm your lawyer, Dawn, not your press agent.

DAWN

Well, get me some of my loungewear then. I can't be on Walter Cronkite looking like this.

DEFENSE ATTORNEY

Did you kidnap Ida Nelson?

DAWN

No! The Dashers did, but they lied. They're just jealous of me because I'm more famous than they are. The Dashers are liars!

DEFENSE ATTORNEY

Well, then, did you strangle your daughter?

DAWN

Yes, I did, and I'm proud of it! If only you could have seen the photos—they were art!

DEFENSE ATTORNEY

You believe the death of your daughter was art?

DAWN

Of course!

(Turning to JURY)

Can't you stupid people see? I'm a huge star! Just pick up the papers and you'll see my picture on the front page. I'm only charged in this matter because I'm so photogenic! I should be on television right this minute.

DAWN starts to model for a disgusted JURY.

DEFENSE ATTORNEY
(Trying to keep Dawn's attention)
What about your nightclub act, Dawn?

DAWN
Ooh, it was a spectacular success! A wild, fast-moving stage show
with a finale to top all finales. They loved it! Even the people that
died loved it. How could they not love dying if they're going to
become famous for it? The jury must realize—look at me! I'm the
most famous person you've ever seen. Take notes while you have
the chance. Quote me! Look at me!
(Throwing her legs up)
Look at my legs! Look at them!

JUDGE
Bailiffs, remove the defendant from the witness stand. Disgusting
display.

The MATRONS drag DAWN from the witness box.

DEFENSE ATTORNEY
The defense rests.

DAWN
(Insanely)
Publicity! The death penalty! Electrocution!!

Dissolve to a stone-faced JURY returning to the jury box.

DAWN is smirking.

JUDGE
Mr. Foreman, has the jury reached a decision?

MR. FOREMAN
(Standing)
We have, your honor. We find the defendant guilty as charged, and
we sentence her to die in the electric chair.

DAWN laughs hysterically.

DONALD and DONNA *pay off IDA in the back row of the courtroom.*

83) *Interior prison. Long shot of rows of cell blocks.*

84) *Interior cell. A REDHEAD PRISONER paces in a rage.*

REDHEAD PRISONER:
Matron! How am I supposed to sleep with these goddamn bugs in here?! Where's that hog?! MATRON, DID YOU HEAR ME?

85) *Interior another cell. CHERYL, a pretty prisoner, is sadly singing alone.*

CHERYL
I come to the garden alone
While the dew
Is still on the roses
And the voice I hear
Ringing in my ear
The Son of God discloses.

86) *Interior yet another cell. DAWN and her hillbilly cellmate, EARNESTINE, are lying on the cot, kissing. Dawn's head is completely shaved and she wears no makeup.*

EARNESTINE
(Crying)
I'm going to miss my little Dawn. It ain't right they can put you in that chair.

DAWN
Oh, Earnestine, I'm thrilled about it. Today is the big day! I feel lucky to receive the death penalty; why, it's the biggest award I could get in my field. God, I don't even have my acceptance speech ready yet—I've *got* to practice it. I know every word I say will be in the newspapers tomorrow. Does it excite you to make love to someone so famous?

EARNESTINE
You excite me, Dawn, not your fame. It's you I love, not all that publicity.

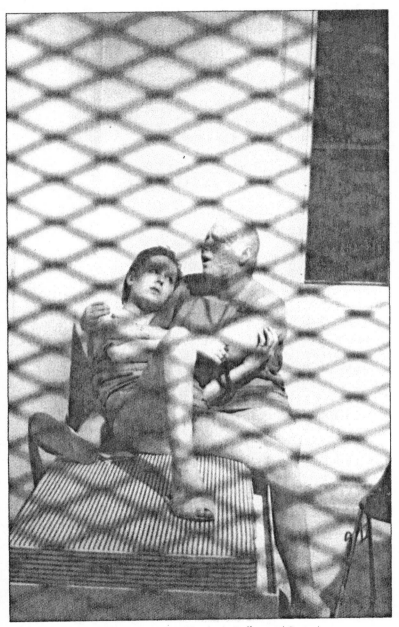

Earnestine and Dawn (Elizabeth Coffey and Divine).

DAWN

I still am the star prisoner, right, Earnestine?

EARNESTINE

Uh huh.

DAWN

Even the warden told me he had trouble with the press trying to get my picture. Will you save my clippings?

EARNESTINE

I'll save them, Dawn. I'll cry when I read them.

DAWN

Will you write a book about me?

EARNESTINE

Uh huh.

DAWN

You know everything; I trust you to write my story. Describe my makeup and hairdos! Include sketches of every outfit I ever wore! Oh, *why* won't they let me wear a gown and makeup today? Today of all days, my big moment in the electric chair . . .

EARNESTINE

You still think you're in a show, baby! You gotta realize it's your life.

DAWN

But my life is a show! Why is it so hard for people to understand. My fans *want* me to die in the electric chair; it will be my final curtain call—the most theatrical moment of my life.

EARNESTINE
(*Hugging her, sobbing*)

Oh, no.

DAWN

I've always tried to be page one, Earnestine. Life imprisonment would be such a second-rate news story. This way my legend will have to live on. I'm not going to die only for my fans of today, but for their children and grandchildren.

EARNESTINE
You're so fucked up, baby! Give mama a big, sloppy kiss.

EARNESTINE and DAWN begin French-kissing passionately.

MATRON A walks into the cell.

MATRON A
Okay LEZBEENS! I caught you! Bumping pussies is a violation of jail rules!

EARNESTINE jumps up in fear.

MATRON A
(Continuing)
I'm going to write this beef up and give it to the warden, Earnestine. You'll get the adjustment center for this.

EARNESTINE
It's her last day, for Chrissake! Can't we spend it together?

MATRON A
Get back to your cell before I beat you to a pulp!

EARNESTINE
(Weeping)
It's her last day, for Chrissake.

The MATRON A shoves EARNESTINE out of the cell.

MATRON A
I know it's her last day! Hahahaha!
(To DAWN)
You all ready for the hot seat, fatso? . . . I'm supposed to ask you what you want for your last meal.

DAWN
I'll have two veal cutlets.

MATRON A

I'll get 'em but you better eat 'em quick 'cause the electric chair
don't wait for nobody!
(Exiting)
You're gonna be one fried lady today!

Dissolve to DAWN alone in her cell, modeling.

CHERYL enters the cell and hugs DAWN.

CHERYL

Dawn, I came to say good-bye. We're going to miss you.

DAWN

Oh, don't look so sad. I'm happy, happy, happy! The only thing I ask
is that you remember me and talk about me the rest of your life.

CHERYL

Oh, we will.

DAWN

And tell everyone they have my permission to sell their memories of
me to the media.

CHERYL
(Overcome with emotion)
Oh, Dawn . . . could I have your autograph?

DAWN
(Getting a piece of paper and pen)
Why, certainly, Cheryl . . .
(Writing)
"To Cheryl:
The prettiest girl on the cell block 4
Love always,
The beautiful and *fabulous* Dawn Davenport."

CHERYL
(Clutching it to her breast)
I'll treasure it.

DAWN

Would you like to see some modeling? I bet you would, and I don't mind.

CHERYL

I'd love to see you perform.

DAWN *begins grotesquely posing.*

CHERYL
(Clapping)
Go! Go Dawn! Go! Go!

MATRON B *enters the cell.*

MATRON B

Get back to your cell, Cheryl! The show's over for Dawn Davenport!

CHERYL

Good-bye, Dawn.

DAWN
(Hugging her)
Good-bye, Cheryl.

MATRON B

Come on, get out of here, Cheryl.

CHERYL *exits.*

MATRON B
(Throwing down dinner plate)
Here's your food, pork chop. Eat up, you ain't got much time.

DAWN

I've changed my mind—I'm really not hungry anymore. Let's not dawdle, I'm all ready for my big news event. I'd like to go right now if it would be alright.

MATRON B

Suit yourself, pizza face.
(Cuffing her)
Let's put your jewelry on.

MATRON A enters.

MATRON A

Here comes the chaplain now. Come on, Miss Star, your time's up!

The CHAPLAIN enters, carrying a Bible.

CHAPLAIN

Are you . . . ready, Dawn?

DAWN
(Excitedly)
Yes, I'm ready, Father. The legend's all ready for her little appointment in the green room. I've been looking forward to this, you know.

86) *Interior prison. Cellblock hallway. DAWN, accompanied by the CHAPLAIN and both MATRONS, takes the long walk toward the electric chair. The other prisoners stick their hands through the bars trying to touch her.*

CHAPLAIN

"The Lord is my shepherd. I shall not want. He maketh me lie down in green pastures . . ."

DAWN

Good-bye, Cheryl!

CHAPLAIN

". . . He leads me beside still waters . . ."

EARNESTINE

Good-bye, Dawn!

DAWN

Good-bye, Earnestine.

EARNESTINE
(Crying)
Oh, Dawn! Good-bye Dawn!

CHAPLAIN
". . . He restoreth my soul . . ."

PRISONERS
Good-bye!

CHAPLAIN
". . . He leads me on the path of righteousness for His namesake . . ."

DAWN
Good-bye, Pat.

REDHEAD PRISONER
Bye, Dawn! Let her go! She's crazy!

CHAPLAIN
". . . Even though I walk through the shadow of death . . ."

87) Interior death chamber. DAWN, MATRONS, and CHAPLAIN enter.

DAWN
(Upon seeing the electric chair)
Hahahaha!

MATRON A
Hop in!

DAWN eagerly jumps into the electric chair while the MATRONS attach the electrodes.

DAWN
Hey, cute . . . it's comfortable, too!

MATRON B
Strap her in good, she deserves worse than this for what she did!

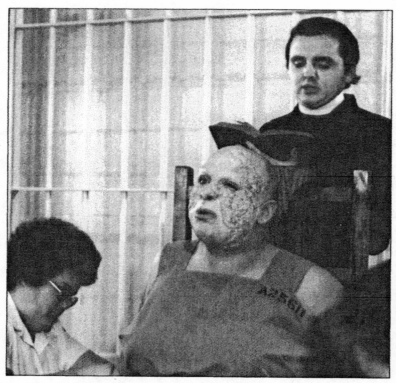

The chaplain (George Stover) blesses Dawn before she gets the chair.

DAWN
(Laughing)
Yeah, you better strap me in good 'cause you don't want me to get
outta here! . . .
(To MATRON A)
HOG! Ha, ha, ha! I HATE YOU! Ha, ha, ha.

MATRON B
Shut up, Davenport.

DAWN is ready for the electrocution. The MATRONS and the CHAP-
LAIN walk away.

DAWN
(Staring insanely into the camera)
I'd like to thank all the wonderful people that made this great moment in my life come true! My daughter, Taffy, who died in order to further my career. My friends, Chiclet and Concetta, who should be with me here today. And thanks to all the fans who died so fashionably and gallantly at my nightclub act. And thank you especially to all those wonderful people who were kind enough to read about me in the newspapers and watch me on the television news shows. Without all of you, my career could have never gotten this far . . .

MATRONS laugh as they get ready to pull the switch.

DAWN
(Continuing)
. . . It is you that I murdered for and it is you that I must die for. Please remember, I LOVE EVERY FUCKING ONE OF YOU . . .

The hideous sound of electricity ripping through Dawn's body is heard. Her whole body becomes stiff and begins twitching obscenely. Smoke comes from the burning flesh under the electrodes.

Freeze frame on Dawn's dying face, her eyeballs bulging and her tongue hanging out. End credits roll superimposed over her face as the title song "Female Trouble" plays faintly in the background.

THE END

A DREAMLAND PRODUCTION

MULTIPLE MANIACS

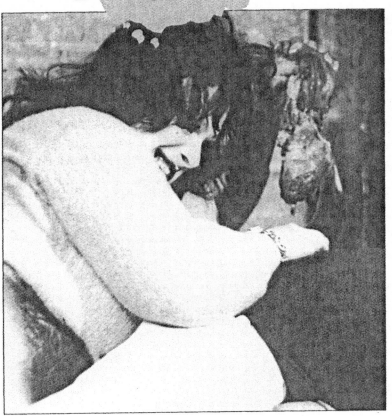

Lady Divine, Mr. David, and his internal organs.

WRITTEN, PRODUCED, DIRECTED, FILMED, AND EDITED BY JOHN WATERS

CAST

LADY DIVINE . . . . DIVINE
MR. DAVID . . . . DAVID LOCHARY
BONNIE . . . . MARY VIVIAN PEARCE
MINK. . . . . MINK STOLE
COOKIE . . . . COOKIE MUELLER
STEVE . . . . PAUL SWIFT
RICKY . . . . RICK MORROW
BARMAID . . . . EDITH MASSEY
JESUS CHRIST. . . . . GEORGE FIGGS
THE INFANT OF PRAGUE . . . . MICHAEL RENNER JR.

WITH SUSAN LOWE, HOWARD GRUBER, VINCE PERANIO, JIM THOMPSON, DEE VITOLO, ED PERANIO, TOM WELLS, GILBERT MCGILL AS "THE FREAKS" AND BOB SKIDMORE, MARGIE SKIDMORE, PAT MORAN, HARVEY FREED, MARK LAZARUS AS "THE STRAIGHT PEOPLE"

1) Homemade credits printed with press type letters on shelving paper unroll onscreen as two notes from rockabilly music blare on soundtrack.

2) Exterior suburban lawn. MR. DAVID, a young man in his twenties, stands on a platform in front of two makeshift tents, barking the show "Lady Divine's Cavalcade of Perversion." He wears a glittery tuxedo and has bleached white hair. Ranch houses are visible in the background.

MR. DAVID
(Using a hand microphone)

Yes, folks, this isn't any cheap X-rated movie or any fifth-rate porno play—this is the show you want; "Lady Divine's Cavalcade of Perversion," the sleaziest show on earth. Not actors, not paid imposters, but real actual filth who have been carefully screened in order to present to you the most flagrant violations of natural law known to man.

3) Interior one of the tents. The ACTORS in the show are getting dressed and killing time before their performance begins. They look dangerous but bored.

SUZIE

Hey, where the fuck are we anyway?

ACTOR A

Timonium, I think.

SUZIE

Gotta match?

ACTOR B

Are we gonna do that pyramid shot like we did yesterday?

ACTOR C

I hope not. I can't take that crap again.

SUZIE

What time's the show start? Hey, where's my blouse?

ACTOR D

Where's Lady Divine? Is she ready?

Lady Divine.

4) Exterior tent. A crowd of SUBURBAN HOUSEWIVES and their SPOUSES have gathered to listen to Mr. David's barking.

> MR. DAVID
>
> These assorted sluts, fags, dykes, and pimps know no bounds! They have committed acts against God and nature, acts that by their mere existence would make any decent person recoil in disgust. You want to see them and we've got them! Every possible thing you can imagine.

More SUBURBANITES approach.

> MR. DAVID
> *(Continuing)*
>
> C'mon ladies! Come right on up this way. Come see "Lady Divine's Cavalcade."

> SUBURBANITE A
> *(To SUBURBANITE B)*
>
> He looks like a fool.

> SUBURBANITE B
>
> Does it cost?

> MR. DAVID
>
> It's absolutely free.

> SUBURBANITE A
>
> Do we have time?

> SUBURBANITE B
>
> We have some time, but I don't know.

> SUBURBANITE A
>
> Oh, come on, it's free.

SUBURBANITES A and B enter the show tent.

> MR. DAVID
> *(To OTHERS)*
>
> Step right up.

David Lochary lures them in.

> WIFE
> *(To her HUSBAND)*
> Do we have time before lunch?

> HUSBAND
> *(To MR. DAVID)*
> This isn't one of those sex shows, is it?

> MR. DAVID
> You'll see, sir. Go right on in.

5) Interior tent. The "show" is already in progress; each little "act" is crosscut with shots of the AUDIENCE shaking their heads in disgust and clucking to one another.

Shot of YOUNG WOMAN sucking a shoe and moaning in erotic pleasure.

Shot of DERANGED YOUNG MAN caressing and sucking a brassiere.

Shot of young girl, SUZIE, with TWO MEN licking her very hairy armpits. SUZIE is nude from the waist up and has lots of tattoos.

"We got it all and we show it all" (Jim Thompson, Susan Lowe, Vincent Peranio)

Shot of NAKED YOUNG MAN being burned with a cigarette by another STRANGE YOUNG MAN in a top hat.

6) Exterior tent. Once again, we see MR. DAVID frantically barking the show. More confused SUBURBANITES have gathered to listen.

MR. DAVID
"Lady Divine's Cavalcade of Perversion," you can still see the complete show. What you will see inside this tent will make you literally sick! We got it all and we show it all! You will witness the actual smut session of a pornographer and his slut of a girlfriend as she, in all her naked depravity, exposes her sacred reproductive organs to the ever probing eye of the flash camera.

7) Interior tent. SUZIE is nude, tilted back on a chair with her legs spread as a PHOTOGRAPHER snaps a close-up of her vagina.

The AUDIENCE is seen reacting with disgust.

SUBURBANITE A
She must be an addict, they'll do anything!

SUBURBANITE B
She's a dyke! Look at those tattoos!

HUSBAND
What's this obsession with pornography?

SUBURBANITE D
Look at her cunt.

SUBURBANITES A and B
(Appalled)
Echhh!

SUBURBANITE E
She's probably got the crabs.

HUSBAND
I can smell her all the way over here.

SUBURBANITE A
God, she guzzled that wine.

HUSBAND
What a repulsive body.

SUBURBANITE B
She's fat.

SUBURBANITE C
No wonder they didn't charge any money to get in here!

A YOUNG MANIAC WOMAN begins mixing in the crowd selling refreshments.

YOUNG MANIAC WOMAN
Cheeseburgers! Get your cheeseburgers! Only a dollar.

SUBURBANITE A
No decent person would be in this show.

SUBURBANITE D

Decent! She doesn't know the meaning of the word decent.

YOUNG MANIAC WOMAN

Cigarettes! Cheeseburgers!

8) Exterior tent. MR. DAVID is bending down to talk to an UNDE-CIDED SUBURBANITE COUPLE still outside the tent.

MR. DAVID

Come on in, you got about three minutes left to catch "The Puke Eater." He'll lap it right up for you, he loves it!

SUBURBANITE F

Sounds weird.

SUBURBANITE F'S WIFE
(To her HUSBAND)

You're weird! It's sickening. I'm not going to Pine Street* just to watch somebody puke.

SUBURBANITE F

Yeah, but they got puke eaters, lesbians, mental patients, and stuff.

MR. DAVID

You'll see two actual queers kissing each other on the lips. These are actual queers!

9) Interior tent. TWO BEARDED MEN French-kiss passionately.

The AUDIENCE is horrified.

ALL
(Gagging, turning their heads in disgust)

Echhh!

SUBURBANITE A

Are they repulsive!!?

---

* The jail for women in Baltimore at that time.

SUBURBANITE B

Filthy!

SUBURBANITE C

But that one looks masculine!

SUBURBANITE A

Yeah, but look at George Hamilton.

SUBURBANITE C

I've known a couple of queers, in fact I think my hairdresser's a queer.

SUBURBANITE D

They hang in bus stations, you know.

SUBURBANITE B

It's just sick.

10) *Exterior tent. Close-up of a frantic MR. DAVID.*

MR. DAVID

See an addicted heroin addict going through the mental and physical agony known as cold turkey! This particular addict has been hooked for over eight years and must constantly lie, rape, mug, and steal from hard-working wage earners in order to satisfy his never-ending crave for hard narcotics!

11) *Interior tent. TWO YOUNG MEN carry out a skinny, emaciated, JUNKIE on a stretcher and dump him on the ground. He moans and rolls around in agony.*

MR. DAVID
(Voice-over)

Watch, as this drug-crazed animal loses all sense of human dignity and decency! He will literally become a maniac before your very eyes.

The JUNKIE finally finds his syringe and shoots himself up, all the while panting and grunting obscenely.

The AUDIENCE reacts smugly.

SUBURBANITE A

God, a needle, yet!

SUBURBANITE D

A filthy one.

SUBURBANITE C

That poor soul!

12) Interior Lady Divine's separate tent. She is stretched out nude, studying her makeup in a small mirror. She is a huge woman with 1940s-style black hair and heavy makeup. Seated on the floor, playing cards, are her two servants, RICKY and GILBERT, who wear bathing suits.

RICKY
(Studying his cards)

Got any fives?

GILBERT hands him a card.

RICKY
(Continuing)

Got any aces?

GILBERT

Go fish.

LADY DIVINE
(Looking up)

Ricky! Ricky!

RICKY rushes over to her.

RICKY

Yes, madame?

LADY DIVINE

Bring me something strong; something I can get off on.

MR. DAVID rushes into the tent.

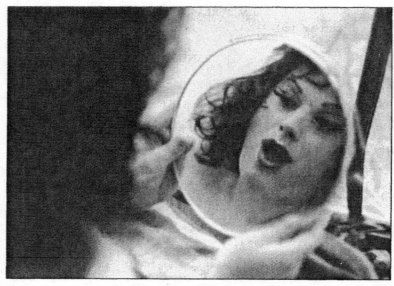

"Maniac" goddess (Divine).

MR. DAVID
(To LADY DIVINE)

You're not ready yet?! Jesus, you come on in a few minutes. Suppose the cops get here? You can't keep this set up . . .

LADY DIVINE

Will you stop badgering me?! My nerves are already a wreck without your nagging! I'm ready—all I have to do is slip into my outfit. We've done this enough times so we don't have to worry about anything happening . . .

MR. DAVID

But the cops! All we need is one porkchop patrolman who starts nosing around. It's gotta be quick . . .

LADY DIVINE

Oh, fuck the cops! They never bust anybody until the show's over and by then . . . . RICKY! Where's my medicine?

RICKY approaches and hands her two black capsules.

LADY DIVINE
(Continuing)
Which ones are these?

RICKY
Your diet medication, madame.

LADY DIVINE
(Taking them both)
Thank you Ricky, darling. Gilbert! Gilbert!

GILBERT approaches.

GILBERT
Yes, madame?

LADY DIVINE
Roll me a few joints before I go on.

MR. DAVID
Roll me one, too.
(To LADY DIVINE)
I can't help but be nervous, all those shit-heads out there . . .

LADY DIVINE
Just relax.

Suddenly a commotion is heard and RICKY and GILBERT drag in a struggling young blond, BONNIE. BONNIE is quite pretty and dressed in heels, pants, and velvet coat.

BONNIE
(Struggling)
Get off! I have to see Mr. David. I have an audition . . .

LADY DIVINE
(Furious)
WHO IS THIS?!

BONNIE
(To MR. DAVID)
I came like you told me, to audition.
(To LADY DIVINE)
And you must be Lady Divine, I've heard so much about you.

LADY DIVINE
Oh, boys, please remove this little slut from my presence immediately!
(To MR. DAVID)
How dare you contaminate my dressing room with this little piece of filth?!

MR. DAVID
She is not. She's an autoerotic, a coprophasiac, and a gerontophiliac and I just thought you might be interested in her for the show.

BONNIE
(Breathlessly)
Yes, I can start immediately. I have this great act worked out with this great old man in his late seventies and this mirror, well, actually he's my uncle but we used to have kind of a thing together and I heard about this show and I thought, what an ideal setup . . .

LADY DIVINE
GET HER OUT OF HERE!

RICKY and GILBERT *drag BONNIE out of the tent.*

BONNIE
Please . . . Please . . .

LADY DIVINE
Just get her out!
(To MR. DAVID)
How can you flaunt your cheap little one-night stands in my face, especially at a time like this?

MR. DAVID
I just thought you might be interested in her for the show.

LADY DIVINE

Well, I'M NOT! I should have pulled those bleached hairs out of her head. You *are* a fool! It's time for my act! Hand me my hose! Be quick!

MR. DAVID

You misunderstand everything I do.

LADY DIVINE

I misunderstand nothing.

13) Interior tent. Wide shot of the "PUKE EATER" doing his "act." He is pudgy, has matted, curly hair, and sits on the floor vomiting into a bucket and then scooping it up with his hands and eating it. Around his neck is a sign reading "The Puke Eater."

The AUDIENCE is horrified. This final act is too much for them and they try to run for the exit but are blocked by MR. DAVID and other ACTORS who are now wielding weapons.

MR. DAVID

Just a minute! And now, ladies and gentlemen, you are going to see something that will make your eyes pop right out of your head! Because of so-called guardians of public decency we are not permitted to describe to you in any way, the hard-core, live, in-person monstrosity we have with us tonight. This sight will be branded in your mind for ever and ever. Anything you may have seen earlier will be a mere warm-up. You are kindly asked to please follow me into our special display room . . .

14) Exterior tent. The terrified SUBURBANITES are led into Lady Divine's tent. They are closely guarded by ACTORS who lurk menacingly nearby carrying sticks, broken bottles, and knives.

MR. DAVID

Right this way! There's no extra charge!

15) Interior Lady Divine's tent. A small curtain hides the next "act." The AUDIENCE is horrified at their predicament.

MR. DAVID

And now, ladies and gentlemen, I can say no more, I give you Lady Divine!

Lady Divine makes herself clear.

The curtains open to reveal LADY DIVINE pointing a gun at the AUDI-ENCE. She wears a skin-tight, wildly patterned dress and looks quite nasty.

LADY DIVINE

Drop 'em boys!

Huge nets fall from the ceiling and entrap the panicked AUDIENCE who begin screaming and struggling.

LADY DIVINE
(Continuing)
QUIET! QUIET WHEN I'M SPEAKING!

As LADY DIVINE speaks, the ACTORS remove the nets from the AUDIENCE. LADY DIVINE points the gun at the crowd the entire time.

LADY DIVINE
(Continuing)
You will not be injured as long as everyone cooperates. Kindly hand over all wallets, jewelry, handbags, any fur items, all loose change, and any narcotics you might be carrying.

SUBURBANITE D
(Terrified)
We'll cooperate!

LADY DIVINE
The first person to give anybody any shit will be immediately eliminated.

SUBURBANITE F'S WIFE
(To the others)
She's sick! We'll never get out of here.

LADY DIVINE
What did you say?!

SUBURBANITE F'S WIFE
(Defiantly)
I said you're sick and repulsive!

LADY DIVINE
And you, my dear, are dead!

She shoots her in the chest. The AUDIENCE screams in terror.

LADY DIVINE
(Continuing)
I SAID NO SHIT AND I MEANT IT! QUIET! Anybody else got any comments?
(To SUBURBANITE E next to dead woman)
How about you, asshole?

SUBURBANITE E
No . . . look . . . please. This girl needs help, she's injured.

LADY DIVINE
She's not injured, honey. She's dead!

JUNKIE
Let's shoot them up with some acid!

LADY DIVINE
That sounds like a good idea, a little something for their brains.
(To AUDIENCE)
Who wants to go on a little trip?
(To horrified SUBURBANITE B)
How about you, honey? Everybody's doing it and I'll be your guide.

Mass panic results. The SUBURBANITES scream and cry in fear as the JUNKIE shoots up SUBURBANITE B.

LADY DIVNE
(Continuing)
Get her! Get her!

SUZIE
(Rifling people's possessions)
Any more pocketbooks around here?
(Grabbing Suburbanite A's arm)
Give me them rings, cunt!

                    LADY DIVINE
                 (To ACTORS)
Got everything? Get her eyelashes! Get that other turd's hairpiece!
                 (More and more hysterical)
I oughta pick off a few more of these shits! Quiet! Quiet!

The SUBURBANITES cringe in awe at Lady Divine's madness.

                    LADY DIVINE
                 (Continuing)
We're going to be leaving you for a while but remember, we have
all your identification papers so we'll know where to find you in
case any of you remember too much when the pigs question you!
You've caught me in a pleasant mood, and you're lucky.
                 (To the ACTORS)
Let's go! Bring the car around!

*16) Exterior Lady Divine's tent. LADY DIVINE, MR. DAVID, RICKY,
and all the ACTORS escape, running through the woods, laughing and
discarding stolen items that did not interest them. Many are still carrying
their weapons.*

                    LADY DIVINE
I oughta go back there and kill 'em!

                      SUZIE
                 (Stopping)
Let's see what we've got.

                    ACTOR A
Any dope?

                    LADY DIVINE
They don't deserve to live!
                 (To ACTORS)
Sit down here and relax.

The ACTORS start looking over more of their stolen items.

                    SUZIE
            (Throwing out some jewelry)
More cheap costume shit.

                   ACTOR B
A box of Norforms!

                   ACTOR C
Here's some diet pills.

                   ACTOR D
Two-fifty! Jesus.

                    SUZIE
I'm tired of getting this trash.
            (Handing ACTOR C a wallet)
Here's some fake I.D for you.

                   ACTOR C
            (Looking through wallet)
What ugly children they have.

RICKY, MR. DAVID, and LADY DIVINE continue walking.

                    RICKY
What'd you get? Don't I get anything?

                 LADY DIVINE
Wait 'til we get back in the car.

BONNIE is hiding nearby in the bushes.

                   BONNIE
Psstt. Mr. David! Mr. David.

                  MR. DAVID
            (Sneaking towards her)
What are you doing here, trying to get us both killed?

*LADY DIVINE and RICKY continue walking, unaware of MR. DAVID
and BONNIE.*

LADY DIVINE

You must be freezing, Ricky darling. Put some clothes on.

RICKY puts on a pair of jeans over his swim suit.

RICKY
(Getting dressed)

Yes, ma'am, it is chilly.

LADY DIVINE

Hurry up. I think I'm beginning to get upset again—my nerves are cracking. I'm getting too old to play this circuit. I'm sick; I'm tired of this show. We just ought to pick them up and shoot them. Fuck all this Cavalcade of Perversion shit; just pick 'em off the street, tie 'em up and kill 'em. We could move a lot faster that way, three or four loads a day. I could get rid of all these tent rentals and all these other people in the show and it could all be MINE to do with as I please.

MR. DAVID is crouching out of sight, talking to BONNIE.

MR. DAVID

I told you to get out of here. I told you!

BONNIE

Mr. David, I have to see you again. I want to perform acts with you, NOW!

MR. DAVID

You know that's impossible.

BONNIE

Oh please, please. God, goddammit.

MR. DAVID

Listen, we'll meet later at Pete's bar on Broadway. You know where it is—around two o'clock.

BONNIE

Yes, I know where it is and I'm going to go there right now and wait. If I have to wait for a hundred hours, I won't budge until I see your face.

Bonnie (Mary Vivian Pearce).

MR. DAVID
(Exasperated)
Just get the fuck out of here.

BONNIE
(Hurt)
Mr. David!

MR. DAVID
I'm only trying to protect you. She's getting worse. Every minute
she's alive she gets worse and worse.

BONNIE
I would risk anything to be with you again.

MR. DAVID
Leave. Go to Pete's.

BONNIE
Hurry to meet me, Mr. David, 'cause I want to perform acts with
you more than anything in this whole world, and it makes me sad
to hear of you being so upset because of that Lady Divine. She's
not a very friendly person but I gotta admit she sure is beautiful
and glamorous, but I bet she couldn't do some of the things we
could do!

RICKY and LADY DIVINE wait impatiently.

RICKY
You'll feel better when we get back to the house.

LADY DIVINE
Where's David?!

MR. DAVID rushes to catch up with them.

LADY DIVINE
(Furious)
Where have you been?

MR. DAVID

Taking a piss, do you mind?

LADY DIVINE

Yes, I mind because I know you're part of it!

MR. DAVID

Part of what?

LADY DIVINE

Trying to purposely get on my nerves—of purposely trying to annoy me! Well, I'm not going to put up with it. Do you think just because I've known you for six years that I won't suspect you of trying to get on my nerves?

MR. DAVID

It's *you* that's getting on my nerves. The whole show is getting on my nerves. We can't do this anymore.

LADY DIVINE

What, are you chicken? Is that it? Lost your nerve?

MR. DAVID

I got better sense.

LADY DIVINE

You're not man enough to stay around with me, baby.

MR. DAVID

I'm not fool enough.

LADY DIVINE

Ah, well then—get lost!

RICKY, MR. DAVID, and LADY DIVINE approach their old white Cadillac convertible, get in, and pull off.

17) Interior moving Cadillac. LADY DIVINE fumes the whole way home as hillbilly music blares on soundtrack.

18) Exterior run-down neighborhood. LADY DIVINE, RICKY, and MR. DAVID exit car, hurry up street toward inner-city row house.

19) Interior row house. LADY DIVINE, RICKY, and MR. DAVID enter a large living room decorated with old furniture, religious statues, and posters for extreme movies—Boom; I, a Woman; *and* Night Games.

MR. DAVID
(To LADY DIVINE)
I just can't stand it. If you don't control yourself a little better, you're not going to make it. It's bad enough doing these things week after week but you're just making it worse for yourself and making everybody else nervous.

LADY DIVINE
I wish somebody'd stop and think about *ME* once in a while. If it wasn't for me, you'd still be back in Boston doing poodle-nappings from those old bitches and if it wasn't for *me*, all the other people in this show'd be still out on the street snatching purses and committing sex crimes and if it wasn't for *me*, you'd be in jail.

MR. DAVID
Do you want a tranquilizer?

LADY DIVINE
I don't *need* any tranquilizers.

MR. DAVID
As far as the police are concerned, you're the one who's going to end up in jail because killing people isn't too bright when we're doing this kind of thing.

LADY DIVINE
I should have killed them all. I wish I could go back there right now and . . .

MR. DAVID
Do you think that makes me afraid of you? Do you think that makes me listen to your ranting and raving? Well, let me make one thing clear, if you can't control yourself a little better, the jig's up and the show's over. The police aren't stupid.

LADY DIVINE

Shit! Aren't stupid?

MR. DAVID

They know we're not stopping. They know the last three shows something happened. You're wanted for murder now, and they usually catch murderers.

LADY DIVINE

Oh, and how about you, Mr. Angel? How about your being an accomplice and how about Sharon Tate? HOW ABOUT THAT!?

MR. DAVID

I told you never to mention that again! I don't remember anything about that, I do NOT remember it, and I won't have you mentioning it.

LADY DIVINE

I just wanted to let you know I hadn't forgotten. Had yourself a real ball that night, didn't you?

MR. DAVID
(Near tears)

Stop it.

LADY DIVINE

Yessiree, a regular little orgy.

MR. DAVID

You were there.

LADY DIVINE

I didn't do what you did.

MR. DAVID

SHUT UP!

LADY DIVINE
(Spelling out with her hands)

P-I-G.

MR. DAVID
(Hands over his ears)
STOP IT!

LADY DIVINE
You're the one who's going to jail. If I go to jail it'll be for other things and I might just start remembering. That's why I'm holding you responsible for what happens to me because if I start remembering, I might have to crack that Tate case for 'em—what have I got to lose?

RICKY
(Bewildered)
Who's Sharon Tate?

LADY DIVINE
(Suddenly calm)
It doesn't matter, darling. Go fix yourself a sandwich.

RICKY
Is there any bologna in there?

LADY DIVINE
Yes, and some cheese—just go ahead and fix yourself a sandwich.

Noises and giggling are heard from upstairs.

LADY DIVINE
(Jumping up)
Cookie? Is that my little Cookie, darling?

MR. DAVID
Why isn't she in school?

LADY DIVINE
'Cause I told her to quit and she did.

MR. DAVID
Is that your idea of a good time, destroying your own daughter?

LADY DIVINE
(Posing in mock terror)
Oh, yes, officer, yes, I have a confession to make—it's about my boyfriend, Mr. David. He's sick, very, very sick, and he's done something very, very bad. Oh PLEASE help him. He did something to the most beautiful girl in Hollywood.

LADY DIVINE laughs cruelly and runs up the steps.

20) Interior Cookie's bedroom. COOKIE, Lady Divine's daughter, jitterbugs with a drainpipe as her nude boyfriend, STEVE, lies in bed smoking a joint. COOKIE wears a pair of shorts and spiked heels and nothing else. Her makeup gives her a bizarrely cheap appearance. LADY DIVINE enters the bedroom.

LADY DIVINE
Cookie! Cookie!

COOKIE
Hey, ma, I was so worried about you—you been gone so long. I'm glad you got back safely. Ma—this is Steve, he's a Weatherman. I met him in D.C. during the riots. Steve, this is my mother, Miss Divine. She's gonna be staying here while she's in town.

STEVE
Hi.

LADY DIVINE
Hello, Steve.

COOKIE
How'd it go today? Did you get me anything?

LADY DIVINE
Oh, yeah, honey, some jewelry and a couple bucks.

COOKIE
I love jewelry.

LADY DIVINE
Had I known you were entertaining, I would have brought something home for Steve. A Weatherman? Well, you must be a very

brave young man. It takes a lot of courage and nerve to do the wonderful things you all do. My little Cookie has excellent taste.

STEVE

Cookie filled me in on your show—sounds great. Did you get any pigs today?

LADY DIVINE

Yeah, honey, a few.

STEVE

Wish I'd of gotten a couple.

LADY DIVINE

Don't be silly, you don't have time for show business. It's more important that you're out there protecting me and my kind of people. It's comforting to know the Weatherman is out there doing his job. I wish I could be that political but I'm so involved with the show but I guess that's doing my part.

COOKIE

Where are Mr. David and Ricky?

LADY DIVINE

Cookie, I've been wanting to talk to you about Mr. David. He's downstairs. He's been getting on my nerves lately and purposely trying to rile me. He's also encouraging insubordination among the other actors.

COOKIE

Kick him out then.

STEVE

Kill his ass.

LADY DIVINE

But then I won't have a boyfriend.

COOKIE

You can find another one, it's real easy. I mean, like Steve here, we just kind of ran into each other.

STEVE

It was weird. This tear gas had gone off and me and this other guy were after this pork we were chasing and Cookie came over with some Vaseline for our faces.

COOKIE

Then we ran down to this clump of bushes next to the Justice Department and made love.

STEVE

And fucked.

COOKIE

We were blinded from the tear gas.

STEVE

We were fucked up anyway from inhaling all this Freon shit and I didn't even know we were in Washington.

COOKIE

Then we went down to this big bank and busted all these windows and lit some fires and then we hitch-hiked home.

STEVE

I've got some good dope, want some?

LADY DIVINE

Oh yes, darling. It might calm my nerves some. I tell you, it does me good to talk to you, at least I know I have a wonderful daughter I can be proud of which is more than I can say for that boyfriend of mine.

STEVE

Want me to go down and hassle his ass for you?

LADY DIVINE

Not in front of Ricky, honey, you'd only upset him.

STEVE
(Handing LADY DIVINE a joint)
Here, have one of these for your nerves.

LADY DIVINE

Oh, thank you.

21) Interior row house living room. MR. DAVID is dialing the phone. A large crucifix sits next to the telephone table.

22) Interior Pete's Hotel bar. A pay phone rings in this shoddy waterfront bar. EDITH the barmaid, an enormous woman with crooked teeth, answers.

EDITH

Pete's . . . yes . . . yeah, there's a blond in here.
> (*Calling out to BONNIE who sits on a bar stool at the other end of the bar*)

Hey, blondie—telephone call.

BONNIE jumps up and runs excitedly to the phone.

BONNIE

For me? Oh, thank you.

The phone call alternates between MR. DAVID at home and BONNIE in the bar.

MR. DAVID

Hello, this is Mr. David. Listen, I'll be there as soon as I can, it's very difficult to get away from here now. Just wait there. I have to talk to you.

BONNIE

Oh, I'll wait right here until you arrive. Yes . . . yes . . . this is a nice club . . . everyone here is treating me so nice . . . I miss you, please hurry.

MR. DAVID

Don't talk to anyone. I'll be there soon.

23) Interior Cookie's bedroom. We see LADY DIVINE nude from the rear as she changes into a skin-tight leopard-skin skirt. COOKIE and STEVE are both partially nude, kissing and fondling one another.

LADY DIVINE
You know, Cookie, Mr. David doesn't really like you.

COOKIE
I don't like him much either.

LADY DIVINE
Ever since we've been going together he uses you to throw up in my face. He says I'm fucking you up.

COOKIE
Well, I'm glad you did! That fart! I couldn't be happier—I have a wonderful apartment, a beautiful mother, and a great boyfriend. Dealing's been good lately too.

LADY DIVINE
You still dealing grass, honey?
            (Struggling to get into skirt)
Here, hook Mom up.

COOKIE
Yeah, still dealing grass and speed when I got it. I almost made two hundred dollars last week and that was a down week.

STEVE
And that beats working, that's for damn sure.

LADY DIVINE
Ain't it?

24) *Interior Pete's Hotel bar. BONNIE is still waiting. EDITH, the bar-maid, approaches.*

EDITH
Would you care for anything else, honey?

BONNIE
No . . . no, thank you.

EDITH
You can't just sit here with nothing to drink.

BONNIE
A Coke then. A Coke will be fine.

EDITH
A Coke it is, then.

MR. DAVID enters the bar.

BONNIE
(Jumping up)
Mr. David!

MR. DAVID
Let's go to this back table.

MR. DAVID and BONNIE sit down at a table.

BONNIE
This is a lovely club.

MR. DAVID
I guess it all depends on your mood.

BONNIE
Aren't you in a good mood?

MR. DAVID
A shaky one. You have no idea what it's been like with her lately—
she's gone completely out of control.

BONNIE
Why was Lady Divine so mean to me today?

MR. DAVID
You don't amuse her, that's all.

BONNIE
Why did you tell me to come, then?

MR. DAVID
I thought she might fall for it.

BONNIE
But I don't have an act for the show.

MR. DAVID
We could have fixed it up.

EDITH eavesdrops from behind the bar.

MR. DAVID
(Continuing)
I think I'm going to leave Lady Divine.

BONNIE
Oh, Mr. David, how wonderful.

MR. DAVID
She'd kill me on the spot if she knew, or have me arrested.

BONNIE
What could she have you arrested for?

MR. DAVID
There's hardly a law I haven't violated.

BONNIE
Why can't we just go to California or Mexico? She'd never find us there and then we could have each other.

MR. DAVID
We wouldn't even get one hundred miles out of town before she'd have the police out.

BONNIE
I don't care where we go! Let's just get a room upstairs so we can perform acts. I feel lonely without you and I miss you and all you ever do is talk about Lady Divine. I hate her! Let's kill her!!

MR. DAVID

Quiet! Keep your voice down. This place is crawling with spies.

EDITH picks up the phone and dials the number for information.

EDITH

Miss Cookie Divine's number please . . . No . . . no, I don't have her
address . . . yes . . . yes . . . 235-2354 . . . Thank you very much.

25) Interior row house living room. LADY DIVINE rushes to answer it.

LADY DIVINE

I'll get it . . . Hello . . . speaking.

EDITH

This is Edith from down Pete's. I don't want to cause you no trouble
or nothing but I thought you would like to know that your old man
is down here with another broad.

LADY DIVINE
(Appalled)
A blond? Thank you very much.

LADY DIVINE hangs up and starts fuming.

LADY DIVINE
(Continuing)
That bastard! I'll get him this time if it's the last thing I do!

COOKIE enters.

COOKIE

What's wrong, mom?

LADY DIVINE

Mother's going out for a while!

COOKIE

Tell me, Mom! What's the matter?

                         LADY DIVINE
That bastard!

                         COOKIE
Mr. David?

                         LADY DIVINE
Yes!

                         COOKIE
Don't worry about a thing, Mom. Just change the locks.

                         LADY DIVINE
I'm afraid it's not that simple, Cookie!

LADY DIVINE exits as COOKIE, with a helpless expression, watches her leave.

26) Exterior row house. LADY DIVINE walks up the slum street. A slow, dirty-sounding instrumental plays on soundtrack as a BLACK CAT crosses her path.

Shot of two GLUE-HEADS stoned in the alley. One is SUZIE, the girl from the Cavalcade, and she looks very rough. With her is one of the ACTORS, he has a beard and is wearing an ugly dress.

The two GLUE-HEADS give each other a repulsed look as LADY DIVINE walks by.

The GLUE-HEADS follow LADY DIVINE and jump her from the rear.

LADY DIVINE struggles but is dragged into another alley by the GLUE-HEADS. Because of Lady Divine's weight it is a difficult task.

The MALE GLUE-HEAD tries to rape LADY DIVINE but finds it difficult due to her dress getting in the way. SUZIE pins Lady Divine's arms to the ground as the MALE GLUE-HEAD paws her. LADY DIVINE struggles and looks repulsed.

Huffin' glue (Howard Gruber, Susan Lowe).

The GLUE-HEADS run away laughing, leaving a stunned LADY DIVINE outstretched in the alley.

Lady Divine's inner monologue is heard in an echoey voice-over during the rest of the scene.

LADY DIVINE

I was in agony. I had been raped before but never in such an unnatural and brutal way. Only because of David's arrogance could those two guttersnipes think they could get away with something like this.

She begins moaning and out of nowhere the INFANT OF PRAGUE* enters, dressed in his original Czechoslavakian costume.

LADY DIVINE
(Continuing)

And then to my horror and amazement the Infant of Prague appeared before me! His angelic gaze hypnotized me—I was dumbstruck! How had he gotten to Bond Street? How did he know I needed him at this very moment? Had God sent him to me as some sort of sign? This could only prove my suspicions of Mr. David's betrayal were not unfounded and my decision to murder him had been approved in the heavens above.

LADY DIVINE and THE INFANT OF PRAGUE begin to walk up the street. LADY DIVINE tries to look holy and glances down at this little saint every so often.

LADY DIVINE
(Continuing)

I took his outstretched hand and let him lead me. I literally put my future into this little saint's hands. He kept mumbling "the more you honor me the more I will bless you." I didn't know what to do! It was the first time in my life that providence had helped me to carry out my plans. He led me for, it seemed, blocks. I could not speak, my head was spinning; I could not believe this had actually happened to me. It was almost as if my guardian angel had revealed himself to me after all these years of uncertainty . . .

---

* A Roman Catholic child saint representing the Infant Jesus.

Michael Renner Jr.'s dad helps the Infant of Prague into his costume.

THE INFANT leads LADY DIVINE to an imposing house of worship.

LADY DIVINE
(Continuing)
. . . He led me to a church, St. Cecelia's, I later found out, as if he meant me to go in. "For what?" I mumbled. To pray?! To mumble a few words of thanks for his help?! To examine my conscience?!

Only now do I realize this great saint had taken me to a church that was to change my life from the moment I stepped into its hallowed halls . . .

THE INFANT OF PRAGUE smiles and walks away. LADY DIVINE nods her head and waves goodbye.

27) Interior Catholic Church. LADY DIVINE enters. She genuflects and lights a candle. Almost no one is around.

> LADY DIVINE
> . . . I went in, not knowing what to expect, and paused to light a candle. Oh Jesus! Oh Mary! Oh St. Joseph! Oh Moses! Thank you for sending a divine messenger in my time of physical and spiritual trouble. Before the Infant appeared to me I felt, what you could even call remorse for the fact that Mr. David's time was obviously up. But now, thanks to your guidance, I realize that one should always follow their own conscience regarding utmost personal matters such as these . . .

LADY DIVINE takes a seat in a pew and makes the sign of the cross.

> LADY DIVINE
> *(Continuing)*
> . . . I took a seat in the back of the church and tried for the first time to make some sort of spiritual contact with my maker. DID HE HEAR ME? Even now I can't be sure but the events that followed in this lovely little chapel can only be described as beyond mortal coincidence. I tried to recall some of the Bible stories I had learned as a child . . .

As LADY DIVINE prays, a religious tableau comes onscreen; JESUS speaks to a CROWD OF FOLLOWERS. The costumes are rather makeshift biblical, and JESUS is played by the same actor who was the JUNKIE in the Cavalcade of Perversion.

LADY DIVINE
(Continuing)
. . . I thought of the time Jesus spoke to a large crowd of devoted
followers who had come to listen to Him preach. I concentrated on
the multitude of sinners gathered here on this holy occasion . . .

*A YOUNG, STRAIGHT COUPLE nervously eyes LADY DIVINE'S
rather animated praying.*

LADY DIVINE
(Continuing)
. . . I realized a young couple was nearby, giggling at me and mocking
my devoted plea but I ignored them for what they were: MERE
FOOLS! CAN'T A DECENT WOMAN EVEN PRAY IN PEACE
WITHOUT MORONS GAWKING AT HER UNASHAMEDLY?
The only way to ignore them was to submerge myself in religious
thought . . .

*We see JESUS holding two fishes and five rolls. The CROWD looks
starved. Suddenly, JESUS raises his hand, a puff of smoke explodes, and
there are hundreds of cans of tuna and many loaves of Wonder Bread.*

LADY DIVINE
(Continuing)
. . . This great story moved me to such great lengths that I tried to
reflect on my own life and its religious connotations. Oh, St.
Matthew! Oh, St. Jude! Oh, St. Cecelia! I honor you with all my
heart and soul but at the same time I find it hard to bow down my
head to you in prayer. My conscience is so immaculately clean that
I fear I nitpick in trying to search my soul for any immoral acts I
may have committed. I can only feel a sort of comradeship to all of
you. I mean, yes, I realize you have lived entirely chaste lives but I,
myself, have done practically the same thing since the days of my
First Holy Communion. I realize that some more uneducated members of the clergy would be quick to point out that I have murdered,
robbed, and whored myself daily but they fail to realize the clear
conscience I have done it all with. Even as I leave this church, I plan
to murder the man who has been closest to me.

Suddenly we see MINK STOLE in rear of church blatently staring at LADY DIVINE. MINK is a religious fanatic dressed all in black with heavy theatrical makeup. She is clutching several rosaries.

LADY DIVINE
(Continuing)

It was about this time I realized my thoughts were not entirely my own. Even as the picture of Christ's great miracle dawned on me, I felt it being sucked out by some unknown presence in this church. I dared not turn around to confront this personality that was robbing me of my pious thoughts and forcing me back into my everyday search for self-gratification at whatever cost possible. I tried to busy my mind in prayer . . .

MINK clears her throat and smiles sexily at LADY DIVINE.

LADY DIVINE
(Continuing)

. . . She coughed, as if to attract attention, and gave me a lewdly religious glare. I realized that I had not discouraged her one bit and continued to pray . . .

Mink Stole *is* the "Religious Whore."

As DIVINE spouts off several "Hail Marys" and "Our Fathers," the religious tableaux begin again. We see JESUS praying and sweating blood as his two, hippyish APOSTLES lie sleeping.

LADY DIVINE
(Continuing)
. . . I realized once again my thoughts were being picked up by the lady behind me. Her presence was everywhere! Again, I tried to rid my mind with prayer . . .

We see JESUS sleeping and the APOSTLES praying. JUDAS approaches, played by the same actor who plays MR. DAVID and kisses JESUS. Suddenly, ROMAN SOLDIERS appear and begin beating JESUS with chains and whips.

LADY DIVINE
(Continuing)
. . . When the apostles saw Jesus was making no use of His supernatural tendencies, they ran for their lives!

We see JESUS being stripped and endlessly beaten in very graphic detail. JESUS vomits blood.

MINK walks up the church aisle, blatantly cruising LADY DIVINE, and takes a seat directly behind her.

LADY DIVINE
(Continuing)
. . . By the time I had picked up a strong sexual vibration from the lady behind me and felt it only proper to move away . . .

LADY DIVINE moves over in the pew but MINK moves to the same pew right next to her. MINK is practically salivating but LADY DIVINE feigns ignorance and continues to pray.

LADY DIVINE
(Continuing)
Not personally enjoying sexual encounters with members of the same sex, I made every possible move to discourage her. She seemed so sure of herself, something I naturally admire in people since I possess this same strong characteristic myself. Although lesbianism

has never really appealed to me, there still was an aura about her that attracted me to her, even in all my distaste for such perversion. After carefully considering it, I decided since the Infant of Prague had brought me to this church I should more or less let fate have its way. I felt if I cooperated with this mysterious woman I could somehow benefit spiritually from the experience. Little did I know what she had in mind.

MINK *begins feeling Lady Divine's leg.*

YOUNG, STRAIGHT COUPLE *flees the church in shocked disbelief.*

> LADY DIVINE
> *(Continuing)*
> I felt her hand reach down and touch my leg, not at all casually. I realized it was too late for social introduction! This lady had a grip on me that even now I find it hard to describe . . .

MINK *begins passionately kissing LADY DIVINE and rubbing a rosary through her hair.*

Filming "The Stations of the Cross."

LADY DIVINE
(Continuing)
. . . She kissed me as if Christ Himself had ordered every move of her experienced tongue. I was suddenly uncontrollable! Although she had only said seven words to me, these words proved to be the key to the most satisfying sexual experience of my entire life!

MINK
Think about the stations of the cross! Think about the stations of the cross!

LADY DIVINE
It was then that I realized she was using her rosary as a tool of erotic pleasure . . .

LADY DIVINE gets into a crawl position and MINK teasingly rubs the rosary all over her while kissing her, then suddenly jams the rosary up Lady Divine's ass.

LADY DIVINE
(Continuing)
. . . My head was spinning . . . and ALL AT ONCE SHE INSERTED HER ROSARY INTO ONE OF MY MOST PRIVATE PARTS!!

MINK jams the rosary in and out as LADY DIVINE moans in pleasure.

Suddenly, the religious hallucinations appear again; this time each one of the stations of the cross is acted out while MINK shouts the matching biblical passages. LADY DIVINE screams in ecstasy.

MINK
Second station—Jesus is made to carry his cross.

JESUS carries the cross while LOCAL TOWNSPEOPLE spit in his face.

MINK
(Continuing)
Third station—Jesus falls the first time.

JESUS falls and hits His head while His crazed ENEMIES throw dirt on him.

MINK
(Continuing)

Fourth station—Jesus meets his afflicted mother.

JESUS greets his MOTHER, played by EDITH, the barmaid.

Long shot of MINK and LADY DIVINE continuing their sexual display in the church.

MINK
(Continuing)

Fifth station—Simon helps Jesus to carry his cross.

A bleeding JESUS is helped by an emaciated SIMON.

MINK
(Continuing)

Sixth station—Veronica wipes the face of Jesus.

VERONICA takes a towel to Jesus' face and the imprint is seen on the towel.

Jesus (George Figgs) falls the first time.

> MINK
> *(Continuing)*
> Seventh station—Jesus falls the second time.

JESUS is bleeding profusely as ANGRY BIBLICAL WOMAN spits right in His eye and He falls again, the cross banging into His head.

LADY DIVINE and MINK writhe passionately. MINK is jamming the rosary with all her might and LADY DIVINE is moaning in pleasure.

> MINK
> *(Continuing)*
> Eighth station—Jesus speaks to the women of Jerusalem.

The WOMEN fall to their knees in front of JESUS.

> MINK
> *(Continuing)*
> Ninth station—Jesus falls the third time.

JESUS falls, almost dead.

> MINK
> *(Continuing)*
> Tenth station—Jesus is stripped of His clothes!

The SOLDIERS strip JESUS and the camera lingers on His skinny body.

> MINK
> *(Continuing)*
> Eleventh station—Jesus is nailed to the cross.

The SOLDIERS hammer nails into Jesus' palms. JESUS screams out in pain.

> MINK
> *(Continuing)*
> Twelfth station—Jesus dies on the cross.

Long shot of crucified JESUS vomiting blood.

Both MINK and DIVINE scream and yell as they climax.

MINK takes the rosary from Lady Divine's ass and wipes it off with a handkerchief. LADY DIVINE fixes her hair and tries to look casual.

A JUNKIE wanders in the church and shoots up on the altar. LADY DIVINE and MINK look disgusted at the JUNKIE and get up to leave.

28) Exterior of church. MINK and LADY DIVINE exit and begin walking.

> LADY DIVINE
> God, it's snowing or something.

> MINK
> Want to get a drink somewhere?

> LADY DIVINE
> Well, no . . . I would, but . . .

> MINK
> Got any money?

> LADY DIVINE
> Not a cent on me.

> MINK
> Can I kind of hang out with you for a while today? I'm supposed to meet somebody up St. Ursula's later but that's not 'til tonight. I don't like to get there too early 'cause I'm heaty up St. Ursula's.

> LADY DIVINE
> I had never done anything like that before, it was wonderful.

> MINK
> Everybody says that once they get into it.

> LADY DIVINE
> I don't even know your name.

> MINK
> It's Mink, but lots of people just call me "the Religious Whore."

LADY DIVINE

Mink, it was a wonderful experience.

MINK

I'm pretty good at it. As a matter of fact, it's the only thing I ever do so I guess I should be pretty skilled by now, huh?

LADY DIVINE

Do you live around here?

MINK

Sometimes. I don't have my own place or anything. I usually sleep in churches . . . in the confessionals. They lock all the churches up now because of thieves and they never check the confessionals. Saturday nights are the only problem and nights before Holy Days because of the early masses the next day and Lent—shit, forget it! I gotta sleep in synagogues then and it's just not the same thing, if you know what I mean.

LADY DIVINE

Yeah.

MINK

What's your name?

LADY DIVINE

It's Lady Divine, but you can just call me Divine.

MINK

I wish I wasn't so heaty! Up Immaculate Conception I almost got caught once and over St. Teresa's they heard about me so they send a nun in to snoop around. I *got* a nun once and let me tell you it was just what she needed!

MINK starts pawing LADY DIVINE.

LADY DIVINE
(Pushing her away, embarrassed)
Please, Mink! People will stare!

MINK
(Hurt)
Hey, I thought we had a thing going.

LADY DIVINE
Oh, we do, Mink, but first I've got to find my husband.

MINK
WHAT?! You've got a husband?!

LADY DIVINE
Actually, he's just my boyfriend but we're through now.

MINK
(Sulking)
Well, I'm going to walk up to . . .

LADY DIVINE
(Grabbing her)
No! Please, Mink, you've got to help me! Come on! I *know* where
he is!

29) *Interior of a sleazy rented room. MR. DAVID and BONNIE are "performing acts." At first, only Bonnie's head is visible and Mr. David's voice
is heard off-screen.*

BONNIE
(Moaning)
Oh, Mr. David . . . this is better than amyl nitrate . . . this is better
than Carbona . . . it's even better than heroin!

MR. DAVID
Go slow . . . turn over!

BONNIE
(Turning to her stomach)
Oh, Jesus! This is better than last time! If only we could perform
acts twenty-four hours a day! Oh, that would be supreme happiness.

BONNIE suddenly begins crying out in orgasm. Mr. David's head slowly comes into view from the bottom of the frame. He picks a hair from his teeth.

> MR. DAVID
> You've been fucking somebody else.

> BONNIE
> No, I haven't, Mr. David, not since last time with you at the movie theater.

> MR. DAVID
> Somebody's been there.

> BONNIE
> Not since we saw *Inga* together, I swear.

> MR. DAVID
> You're lying.

> BONNIE
> How could I? I had never had an experience like that before.

> MR. DAVID
> Well, somebody has!

> BONNIE
> No, I swear . . . well, no MAN has. No one has been near my private parts except for this old lady I met on the bus.

> MR. DAVID
> I knew it.

> BONNIE
> It was just that she was so old I felt bad for her. I only let her . . . well, you know . . . it was no big production or anything, it *was* on the bus and all.

> MR. DAVID
> *(Smiling)*
> It's almost better than what we did at *Inga*.

> BONNIE
Nothing could be better than that, Mr. David.

> MR. DAVID
Do you remember that usher?

> BONNIE
> *(Giggling)*
Do you think he saw us?

> MR. DAVID
Well, he saw the dildo!

BONNIE goes down on MR. DAVID off-screen.

> MR. DAVID
> *(Writhing)*
You do it better than anybody!

> BONNIE
Performing acts is my specialty. Turn over!

30) Exterior slum street. LADY DIVINE and MINK are still walking. Startled PASSERSBY turn their heads to stare.

> LADY DIVINE
He's going to regret having ever met me once I get ahold of him. C'mon Mink. That slimy little pigfucker! He should be dead right this minute and that little hussy oughta be buried right next to him. He's done his last show with "The Cavalcade of Perversion."

> MINK
"The Cavalcade"?! Oh, wow! Are you from "The Cavalcade of Perversion"? I read about that in the morning paper.

> LADY DIVINE
I run it, baby. It's my show.

> MINK
Oh, Jesus. You're my first celebrity I ever gave a rosary job to, and at St. Cecelia's! Wow, imagine!

LADY DIVINE

I can tell you, the master of ceremonies is about to be eliminated.

MINK

How? Are you going to do it?

LADY DIVINE

Yes, I am!

MINK

Oh, please let me come! Please! I've wanted to perform Extreme Unction on someone all my life. I'll do anything you ask but please let me come.

LADY DIVINE

I don't give a shit who comes. All I know is once I find him I'm going to make sure he doesn't walk out of that room alive. I don't care if you throw a party for it. I wish I had a chance to call all of my friends and invite them over to watch. I wish I had a movie camera so I could record every second of it so afterwards I could just sit and gaze at all my lovely work. And that GIRL—that cheesy little streetwalker. Neither one of them deserve an ounce more oxygen running through their putrid little lungs. I hope they've had their fun because it'll be the last fun they ever experience.

MINK

Oh, a double ceremony! Oh, Lady Divine, this will be my supreme day on earth! I've wanted to perform Extreme Unction on someone since I was seven years old. And now, not only one body to bless but two! Lady Divine . . . you're going to make me a very happy girl.

31) Interior sleazy rented room. MR. DAVID and BONNIE are relaxing in bed smoking a cigarette.

BONNIE

Mr. David, am I better than Lady Divine?

MR. DAVID

Different. Just completely different.

BONNIE

Yeah, I guess Lady Divine is what you men call a real piece.

MR. DAVID

She's lost all her sex appeal.

BONNIE

Does she love you?

MR. DAVID

She used to, but now she's incapable of even *liking* anyone.

BONNIE

I don't even want to think about her. She's keeping us apart.

MR. DAVID

She didn't used to be such a monster. When I met her in 1963, she was just an ordinary shoplifter with lots of fun inside.

BONNIE

What were you, though?

MR. DAVID

Oh . . . I was unemployed. I always was 'til I met her. She taught me all the ropes; dog-napping, phony credit cards, blackmail, swindling, drug dealing. But then she got really shaky—she became so hostile; you couldn't depend on her to just pull off a job—no, she'd always have to stick around and rough them up. Then she got really bad—she killed a cop, it was really stupid. He was just standing there, directing traffic, and she was in a particularly shitty mood. She had a new Eldorado then, she was making good money. He was standing there and she just headed right for him, floored it, and ran him right down. Why we didn't get nailed for that one, I'll never know. It was awful, she flattened him like a pancake—school children were around, screaming . . . she just laughed and went on. We heard the ambulance sirens but she just reached over and turned up the radio. It made her happy; she loved it. From that day on, if she gets to kill a cop, it's one of her most satisfying days.

BONNIE

Didn't anyone get your plates?

MR. DAVID

I don't know; she abandoned the car the next day.

BONNIE

Oh, Mr. David, I can't think of anything but to kill her!

MR. DAVID

We're together now, aren't we?

BONNIE

But I mean living together, day in and day out.

MR. DAVID

You see, I'm afraid of her. If she found us, she'd kill us both.

BONNIE

Then it would be self-defense, we'd have to.

MR. DAVID

Bonnie . . . have you ever killed anyone before?

BONNIE

No, I haven't. But it would be something new—something to prove how much I love you; a gift from me to you.

They kiss.

MR. DAVID

How would we do it?

BONNIE

Haven't you ever killed anyone?

MR. DAVID

Well, I've been with Lady Divine many times when she has. It used to upset me but I have to let her do it now . . . she claims I did once but I can't remember anything about it. We were in Hollywood . . . and . . . Oh, Bonnie, I don't like to talk about it.

BONNIE

Oh, Mr. David, I'm sorry. But if you had killed someone you would remember it.

MR. DAVID

I honestly can't.

BONNIE

Then I'll do it all by myself. It's the only way I have to prove to you how much I cherish our relationship.

MR. DAVID

If you did that for me, I could never ask another thing from you.

MR. DAVID kisses her.

BONNIE

Then it's settled.

MR. DAVID

Get dressed. We'll have to do it now or I'll lose my nerve.

BONNIE

Okay.

MR. DAVID

She'll be home . . . we can go there . . . you wait outside the door, I'll leave it unlocked—I'll go in and try to make love to her. You'll have the gun . . . I'll cough, that's your signal . . . you come in, I'll jump up and you shoot her. We'll just leave her there. She's wanted for so many murders the police won't even care who killed her. But Bonnie . . . you have to do it. I realize I'm as guilty as you are but I just can't do it.

BONNIE

It sounds fantastic. Let's go there right now! Will anyone else be there?

MR. DAVID

Cookie, her daughter. But she goes out eventually, she goes out every day. She's a whore, just like her mother.

BONNIE

Mr. David, after this is all over, I'm going to show you what happiness is all about! Where would you like to go? California? Mexico? We'll lead a life of constant acts performed to perfection!

MR. DAVID
(Kissing her)
I love you so fucking much I could shit.

32) Exterior of Pete's Hotel bar. MINK and LADY DIVINE walk down the street.

LADY DIVINE
This is the place.

MINK
Pete's? I was there once, a lot of hippies go there.

Lady Divine demands answers from Edith (Edith Massey).

LADY DIVINE

Yeah? Well, I know of two who are going to be leaving real soon!

LADY DIVINE bangs angrily on the door.

MINK

Suppose no one answers?

LADY DIVINE

I'll kick the door in.

LADY DIVINE continues knocking impatiently. EDITH, the barmaid, finally answers.

EDITH

Hold on, hold on . . . Oh, it's you, Lady Divine.

LADY DIVINE

Where are they?

EDITH

They left fifteen minutes ago.

LADY DIVINE
(Grabbing EDITH)

Are you lying to me?

EDITH

I ain't lying, I called you, didn't I? They took a room upstairs. I thought you'd be here sooner.

LADY DIVINE

I had some complications.

EDITH
(Looking off-screen)

Uh, oh. We got company.

A COP approaches.

COP

Okay, girls, let's have some I.D. papers. Got something for me today, Edith?

EDITH
(Fumbling in her pockets)

Oh yes, yes.

(Giving the COP a bill)

That's all I have today is a twenty.

COP

You better get the rest to me soon.

EDITH
(Scared)

I'll have it at the end of the week.

LADY DIVINE
(To COP)

What'd we do?

COP

Let's see the I.D. I don't recognize you girls from around this neighborhood. We don't like your kind around here much so if you know what's good for you, you won't be walking the streets.

LADY DIVINE

Suppose you let me make up my mind for myself, okay copper?

COP

Get smart with me lady I'll run your ass in.

MINK
(Trying to be polite)

I don't have any I.D. papers, officer, but we didn't do anything.

COP

Yet, you mean. I know your type; you're lezbeen hookers an' we don't like no lezzies in this neighborhood so if you're smart, you'll get on a bus and go uptown or wherever you came from.

LADY DIVINE

Hey, you're talkin' to a lady! You better watch your language, pig, before I turn you into a piece of bacon!

She grabs Mink's arm and they walk away.

LADY DIVINE
(Over her shoulder to COP)
Why aren't you out catchin' criminals and murderers?

33) Interior row house living room. COOKIE wears only a pair of shorts and sits on the floor next to the couch. RICKY is sprawled out on the couch smoking grass through a waterpipe.

COOKIE
I'm worried about Mother.

RICKY

For what?

COOKIE

That shit-head Mr. David's giving her trouble. I told her to get rid of him. He's an asshole! She doesn't need the aggravation; she's not herself lately. I mean, she's always jumpy, but not this bad.

RICKY
All I can say is I wish somebody'd give me my pay.

COOKIE

She'll pay ya.

RICKY

But when? She made plenty in D.C. last week and she didn't give me a penny.

The sound of a door slamming is heard off-screen.

COOKIE
(Jumping up)
Maybe this is Mom . . . Mom?

MR. DAVID enters.

MR. DAVID

Where's your mother?

COOKIE

She's out and what do you care?

MR. DAVID

Don't be smart, remember who you're talking to.

COOKIE

And who's that?

MR. DAVID

Your mother's boyfriend and don't forget it.

COOKIE

I think Mother's forgotten it!

On location in John Waters's real apartment (David Lochary, Cookie Mueller, Rick Morrow).

MR. DAVID

What's that supposed to mean? And Ricky, what do you think you're doing?

RICKY

Lying here on the couch, relaxing, and taking dope.

MR. DAVID
(To COOKIE)

Don't you ever wear clothes anymore or are you some kind of nudist? You had one trick earlier, wasn't that enough? Really, your mother's employees!

COOKIE

Oh, get out of my face, will you? Remember, this is my home and I'm being gracious enough to let you stay here. If you ever came to my door alone, I wouldn't even answer it.

MR. DAVID

I wonder how your mother would appreciate this kind of behavior? Lying around all day, screwing anything that's handy, taking dope constantly, and stealing and whoring in the streets nightly!

COOKIE

I haven't heard any complaints from mother. As a matter of fact, I think she's quite happy with the way I'm conducting myself. She told me she thought I was a very brave and charming young lady and she also told me that she had it with you—you get on her nerves—excess baggage! She's out right this minute looking for you to tell you and I'll laugh my ass off when I see your face after she's through.

RICKY

All I can say is I wish somebody'd give me my pay.

MR. DAVID

Well, nobody's going to so why don't you just get your clothes on and get out? Huh? What'd you think of that?

RICKY

I think you ought to keep your fucking mouth shut.

MR. DAVID

Don't say "fuck" to me!

RICKY

(Jumping up and grabbing MR. DAVID)

Look Mr. Fag Man, you didn't hire me and you're not going to fire me!

COOKIE

(Breaking up the fight)

Calm down! Calm down! Sit down!

(To RICKY)

You'll get your pay!

(To MR. DAVID)

I oughta let him rip your ass apart. We'll SEE who gets fired! Mother doesn't make many mistakes in her life, but when she does she sure picks a lemon. God, you make me puke!

(Losing control)

This is my house! I'm trying to respect my mother's wishes! I hope she changes her mind about a few people, AS I SUSPECT SHE WILL!

The director zooms in.

MR. DAVID
(To RICKY)
What's "Mr. Fag Man" supposed to mean?

RICKY
Just keep your fucking mouth shut, alright?

MR. DAVID
Even if I was a fag, which I'm sure you realize is NOT the case, you would be my very last choice as a mate, even Liberace would be more appealing to anyone with the particular neurosis you so rudely attribute to me.

The slaughter begins.

COOKIE
(Putting on her coat to exit)
Oh, you're both horrible and disgusting. I hope you're not here
when I get back, I don't ever want to ever see your faces again.
(Sobbing)
I hate you! You've driven me from my own home!

*COOKIE exits and a gunshot is heard. COOKIE staggers back into the
apartment and collapses; she has been shot in the face. BONNIE runs in,
holding the smoking pistol.*

BONNIE
(Scared)
Mr. David! She saw me, I had to!

RICKY has jumped up and tries to escape.

MR. DAVID
(To BONNIE)
Aim at him! Aim at him!

BONNIE points the gun at RICKY.

BONNIE
(To MR. DAVID)
I thought it was her! She saw me, she looked me right in the eye!

MR. DAVID
Just aim the gun at him.

BONNIE
Should I kill him too?

MR. DAVID
If he tries anything, shoot him.

RICKY
(Holding his hands in the air)
What are you people doing?

MR. DAVID
(To RICKY)
Being awfully polite now, aren't you?
(Shoving him to the floor)
Get your head down!
(To BONNIE)
Tie him up and gag him good.
(To RICKY)
Don't move an inch or she'll shoot your brains out!

BONNIE *gives MR. DAVID the gun to cover RICKY. She gets some rope and begins tying RICKY up.*

BONNIE
(To MR. DAVID)
I'm sorry, I know it was dumb but I saw her and she scared me. Who is she?

MR. DAVID
Divine's daughter.

BONNIE
I feel kind of bad about it but everything will be all right, won't it?

MR. DAVID
Hurry up! She'll be home any minute. We've got to hide them.

MR. DAVID *and BONNIE begin moving RICKY, bound and gagged, to a hiding place behind the couch.*

34) *Exterior alley. MINK and LADY DIVINE loiter.*

LADY DIVINE
That pig cop called us *lesbians!*

MINK
Cops are always hassling me. Just 'cause I'm pretty, they think I'm a whore. As far as being gay, how long have you been a lesbian?

LADY DIVINE

Gay!? I'm no lesbian . . . at least not until a little while ago—you're
the first female I ever did anything with.

MINK

I'm glad I was the one. I bet your boyfriend will be mad.

LADY DIVINE

Who knows what that moron will think! I can't even think straight
after that copper. I tell ya, Mink, I got one once. It was a real kick!
I ran him down in my Eldorado. And then there was another one,
one time back in California—he gave me a warning ticket but I
wouldn't take it—last goddamn warning ticket he ever gave. But
you know. I never got one with my bare hands and I'd sure like to.

MINK

I just tried to be nice so we could get away from him. I think they
have my description in one of their files; it's getting so I can't even
step in a First Friday service without somebody getting uptight.
Can't we go now? You had me all worked up thinking I could perform Extreme Unction on your boyfriend and his date!

LADY DIVINE

Don't you worry yourself about that, honey! We'll get 'em! We'll go
back to my daughter's place—they'll be there alright.

MINK

But who will you say I am?

LADY DIVINE

My new girlfriend, Mink.

They kiss passionately.

MINK
(Looking up)
Here comes that copper again.

COP enters.

COP

I thought I told you two to beat it.

LADY DIVINE
(Being overly polite)
Officer, we're trying to leave but we can't find the bus stop, we're lost. Will you help us?

COP
(Pointing)
It's up Broadway.

LADY DIVINE
(Pointing the other way)
I thought it was up that way.

COP
(Turning his back to her)
Up where?

LADY DIVINE
Up there.

LADY DIVINE grabs him around the neck and starts strangling him.

MINK
(Jumping up and down)
Get him, Divine, GET HIM!

LADY DIVINE
Help me!

MINK begins kicking the COP as LADY DIVINE continues strangling him. Finally, the COP loses consciousness, and they let him collapse in the street.

LADY DIVINE
(Continuing)
Ha! Just like ropin' hogs, ain't it, hon? Come on, we got two more dead creeps waitin' up at my place.

They walk up the street laughing.

35) Interior row house living room. MR. DAVID and BONNIE are hiding Cookie's bloody corpse behind the couch.

BONNIE

Let's put her back here.

MR. DAVID
(Struggling)
God, we have to go through with it now, if Lady Divine sees this she'll die—she'll be foaming at the mouth.

BONNIE
This excites me, Mr. David. Does it excite you?

MR. DAVID

In what way?

BONNIE

You know.

MR. DAVID
Don't you ever think of anything else?

BONNIE

Yes, but it's all boring.

MR. DAVID
Make sure there is no blood around.

BONNIE

Get me a rag.

MR. DAVID gets the rag.

MR. DAVID
(Wiping up blood)
We've got to hurry.

As they clean, MR. DAVID picks up a newspaper and sees the headline. He is quite shocked.

MR. DAVID
(Continuing)
"Arrest Weirdo in Tate Murder." God, she was lying the whole
time! The whole thing—that cruel bitch!
(Reading from newspaper)
"Charles Watson, Patricia Krenwinkle, Charles Manson." I never
heard of these people! That lying bastard!

BONNIE

Lying about what?

MR. DAVID

Sharon Tate.

BONNIE

You knew her?

MR. DAVID

Oh, God, Sharon Tate!

The front door slams.

MR. DAVID

God, she's home!

BONNIE
(Nervously)
What should I do, tell me, Mr. David!

MR. DAVID
(Giving her the gun)
I'll cough—that's your signal.

BONNIE
(Putting the gun under a pillow on her lap)
I'm nervous, Mr. David, but it's all for you. It's all for you.

LADY DIVINE and MINK stomp into the living room.

LADY DIVINE
(To MR. DAVID and BONNIE seated on couch)
Where's COOKIE?!

MR. DAVID
She went out.

LADY DIVINE
Out where?

MR. DAVID
Just out, that's all.

LADY DIVINE
That's a lie!
(Pointing to BONNIE)
Why do you bring these sluts to my daughter's apartment? That's not very polite.

MR. DAVID
I notice you're not alone.

LADY DIVINE
Yeah? What you got to say about that?

MR. DAVID
Nothing, I'm just rather surprised at your taste.

MINK
And what's that supposed to mean?

MR. DAVID
(Flippantly)
Take it for what it's worth.

LADY DIVINE
Not much, coming from a shit like you. This happens to be Mink Stole, she's going to be traveling with me for a while.

MR. DAVID
So you finally turned dyke, I'm not surprised.

LADY DIVINE

Dyke?!
(Pointing to MR. DAVID)
Look who's talkin', all peroxided up!
(Pointing to BONNIE)
And what's with her? Is she some kind of mute?

BONNIE

I can talk.

LADY DIVINE

Well, say something real cute then, honey.

BONNIE

Lady Divine, there's no reason for us to be mean to each other. Mr. David and I are in love and you have someone else too, so there's no reason for any hard feelings.

LADY DIVINE

Oh God, she can talk. How unfortunate.
(To MINK)
Sit down, Mink, make yourself comfortable, I've got something to tend to in the kitchen.

MINK sits down and gives MR. DAVID and BONNIE a snotty look as LADY DIVINE exits to kitchen.

MR. DAVID

I hope you two will be very happy together.

MINK

Yeah? Well, I don't like people calling me a dyke when it's obvious . . .
(Looking at BONNIE)
. . . that you have extremely perverted tastes yourself.

BONNIE

Mr. David, I can only take so much of this kind of talk, especially from a common lesbian!

MINK

Well, my dear, at least I'm not a bleach-blond hussy that goes around screwing unhired gigolos.

MR. DAVID
(To MINK)

Quiet! Remember, you're speaking to someone miles above your element. Where did Lady Divine meet you? On the streets? Or were you her gym instructor?

MINK
(Yelling to DIVINE)

Lady Divine, this asshole is getting awful disrespectful to me and his scummy little girlfriend too! I mean, I can only sit around here and be insulted by turds for so long! Everybody has a limit!

LADY DIVINE re-enters the living room. In one hand behind her back is a butcher knife. She hands MINK a bottle of Wesson oil.

LADY DIVINE
(To MR. DAVID)

Where's Ricky?

MR. DAVID

He quit.

LADY DIVINE

That's a lie!

BONNIE

He quit because you still had not paid him.

LADY DIVINE

WAS I TALKING TO YOU, MISS?!

MR. DAVID

He demanded money from me, I wouldn't give it to him and he left.

LADY DIVINE

Oh, you fired him and you know it! Maybe you can pull this shit over on this little trick, but I'm Lady Divine, just remember that!

BONNIE
(Jumping up with the gun)
At least I'm not a fat hog like you!!

LADY DIVINE
(Enraged, running at her with butcher knife)
OH GOD!!

MR. DAVID
Shoot her! Shoot her!

Before BONNIE can shoot her, LADY DIVINE stabs her in the chest as MR. DAVID screams in horror.

LADY DIVINE stabs BONNIE repeatedly and laughs hideously.

LADY DIVINE
(To MR. DAVID)
You're next!
(To MINK, giving her Bonnie's gun)
Take this and cover me!

MINK
(Holding the oil)
Can I do it now?

LADY DIVINE

Do anything you like! She's all yours but hurry because pretty soon you'll have a backlog of work to do.

MINK begins blessing BONNIE'S corpse with oil and mumbling while performing the sacrament of Extreme Unction.

MR. DAVID
(Cringing in terror)
Divine, think what you're doing!

LADY DIVINE
(Advancing on MR. DAVID with butcher knife)
You knew she had that gun! You were going to let her kill me!
Couldn't do it yourself, you slimy coward.

MR. DAVID
You can't scare me anymore. I know about Sharon Tate. They
arrested three people in California for killing her and I didn't even
know them!

LADY DIVINE
Maybe they got the wrong people.

MR. DAVID
It's the right people, it's headlines!

LADY DIVINE
Yeah? Well, I don't see where that makes much difference now! I
mean, SO WHAT?! In a minute I'm going to dismember you in
front of your very eyes! I wonder how it'll feel to be hacked to
pieces with a butcher knife? Think it'll hurt?

MR. DAVID
(Pleading as the knife gets nearer his throat)
Be human! Six years! You can't wipe it out that easy!

LADY DIVINE
I'm having no trouble.

MR. DAVID
Please . . . Oh, God.

MINK
I'm finished. Is he ready yet?

LADY DIVINE
NOW HE IS!

*LADY DIVINE stabs MR. DAVID repeatedly in the chest and throat, all
the while smiling and laughing. She rips out his heart and liver and
caresses it in her hands. Finally, she laughs grotesquely and stuffs the heart*

into her mouth and eats it. She gags as she chews and blood oozes from her mouth.

MINK rushes over to Mr. David's Corpse with her bottle of oil.

MINK

Oh, Divine, what a wonderful afternoon! You can't imagine what it's like for me—it's like fucking Jesus! Performing Extreme Unction is practically the most erotic and stimulating thing I can imagine.

LADY DIVINE

Look, Mink, he's just meat now, common ground beef! And he deserves it! God, I love that feeling when the knife goes in and resists a little, after that it's almost a letdown.

MINK
(Blessing Mr. David's body)
Isn't there anybody else we could do it on? I'm all worked up.

LADY DIVINE
There's nobody left, NOBODY!

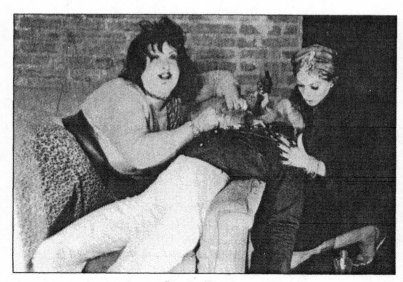

Extreme Unction.

MINK

We could find someone.

LADY DIVINE

Who, though, who?

MINK

God, there are hundreds of people I have in my fantasies: Ann-Margret, Tricia Nixon, Shirley Temple, THE POPE!

LADY DIVINE

Oh, Mink, we could go on for days: Ronald Reagan and his family, the entire Baltimore City Police Force, and BARBRA STREISAND!

MINK

This will be a day I can never forget! I have experienced *raw* happiness!

Suddenly RICKY makes a noise from behind the couch and lurches out trying to free himself of his restraints. MINK screams and shoots him in the head.

LADY DIVINE
(Screaming)
YOU FOOL! YOU FOOL IDIOT! YOU'VE KILLED RICKY!!

MINK
(Running from LADY DIVINE)
I didn't know! He scared me! I swear, I thought he was one of them!

LADY DIVINE
(Advancing on MINK with her knife)
YOU KILLED HIM, the only person who didn't betray me!

MINK
(Falling to her knees as LADY DIVINE nears her)
Don't make me shoot you. PLEEAASE!

LADY DIVINE

YOU KILLED HIM!

LADY DIVINE *stabs* MINK *several times and leaves the knife stuck in her head. Once again, LADY DIVINE starts laughing and suddenly begins foaming at the mouth. The white foam pours down onto her sweater as she staggers over to a full-length mirror and begins talking to herself.*

LADY DIVINE
(Continuing)

Oh, Divine, you're still beautiful! Nothing that has happened can change that! I love you, I love your sickness, I love your crimes, I love your murders! Oh, Divine, I love your twisted mind. I love you so much and you're still the most beautiful woman in the world! Nothing can change that! And now, you're a maniac but what a wonderful state of mind that can be! How exciting! How stimulating! And now you're alone the way it should be, the way it will be!

Out of the corner of her eye, she spots a portion of Cookie's bloody dress behind the couch. She rushes over and sees her daughter's body and begins screaming and crying.

LADY DIVINE
(Continuing)
COOKIE! OH GOD! COOKIE! COOKIE!

LADY DIVINE, *crying hysterically, holds* COOKIE *in her arms.*

She staggers to the front of the couch and collapses. Her eyes are dazed and she has obviously completely flipped out.

LADY DIVINE
(Continuing)

You're finally there, Divine, and you don't ever want to go back. I have to go out now, I better change.

LADY DIVINE *exits to bedroom.*

Camera silently pans over the corpses in the living room.

LADY DIVINE *returns in a one-piece white swimsuit and a full-length mink coat. She falls to the couch and begins talking to herself.*

LADY DIVINE
(Continuing)
Oh, Divine, you have to go out in the world in your own way now. You know it's all right, you know no one can hurt you. You have x-ray eyes now and you can breathe fire. You can stomp out shopping centers with one step of your foot, you can wipe out entire cities with one blast of your fiery breath. You are a monster now and only a monster can realize the fulfillment I am capable of feeling. Oh, Divine, it's wonderful to feel this far gone, this far into one's own depravity! I am a maniac; a maniac that cannot be cured! Oh, Divine, I AM DIVINE!

A huge, twenty-foot broiled LOBSTER appears out of nowhere and begins attacking LADY DIVINE. She screams and attempts to fight him off but the LOBSTER lunges on top of her and begins raping her. LADY DIVINE screams and struggles but is overpowered by the LOBSTER.

LADY DIVINE
(Shrieking in agony)
LOBSTORA!!

Finally, the LOBSTER pulls off and disappears as fast as it entered the scene. LADY DIVINE lays dazed, her crotch bloodied by the attack.

LADY DIVINE falls to the floor, completely out of her mind, and stares directly into the camera, eyes rolling in her head. She breaks into an insane laugh and crawls out the front door onto the street.

36) Exterior row house. LADY DIVINE begins prowling her neighborhood and spots a HOUSEWIFE stopped at a stop sign in a station wagon. As intense classical music plays on soundtrack, LADY DIVINE tries to rip open housewife's car door. HOUSEWIFE tries to lock herself in but isn't quick enough. LADY DIVINE opens the front door and pulls out bags of groceries, throwing them into the street. LADY DIVINE pulls the terrified HOUSEWIFE out of her car, jumps into the driver's seat, and pulls off.

37) Exterior suburbia. LADY DIVINE drives the stolen car into the country. The ground is snow-covered.

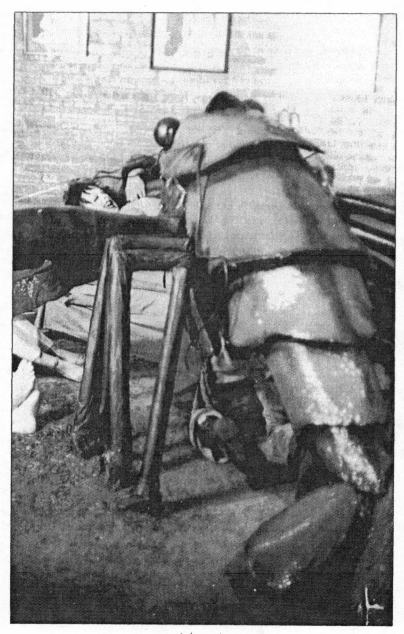

Lobstora!

She parks the car and begins walking in the deep snow, despite the fact she is wearing only a pair of black heels, a bathing suit, and her mink coat.

She approaches suburban ranch houses and peers into the windows.

38) Exterior Lover's Lane. A YOUNG COUPLE is parked drinking beer and making out. LADY DIVINE attacks the car with a mallet she has found and the YOUNG COUPLE flees the car. LADY DIVINE breaks all the windows with the mallet.

39) Exterior downtown Baltimore. We see LADY DIVINE come around a corner and begin to attack PASSERSBY. PEOPLE begin running.

The whole street is filled with PANICKED CITIZENS trying to escape the human monster, LADY DIVINE.

LADY DIVINE waves her arms and growls like a monster.

THE NATIONAL GUARD appears and surrounds her as the cheering CROWD shouts their encouragement.

The government to the rescue.

LADY DIVINE screams and struggles but is shoved to the ground by the GUARDSMEN. Patriotic music begins playing on soundtrack.

THE GUARDSMEN raise their rifles and take aim.

The CROWD cheers wildly for her death.

The GUARDSMEN begin to pump Lady Divine's massive body full of bullets.

Close-up of Lady Divine's distorted, mutilated face as she finally succumbs to society's rigid rules.

THE END.